DEBATE Pro

Book 1

Author Jonathan S. McClelland
- BA in English with a Writing Concentration, University of South Carolina, Columbia, SC, USA
- Former English instructor at Daewon Foreign Language High School
- Current debate instructor for elementary school students
- Former curriculum developer at Korean Army Intelligence School
- Expert test developer of TOEFL, TOEIC, and TEPS

DEBATE Pro Book 1

Publisher Chung Kyudo
Editors Hong Inpyo, Cho Sangik
Proofreader Michael A. Putlack
Designers Zo Hwayoun, Park Sunyoung
Illustrator Kim Seyoung

First Published in May 2013
By Darakwon, Inc.
Darakwon Bldg., 211, Munbal-ro, Paju-si, Gyeonggi-do 10881
Republic of Korea
Tel: 82-2-736-2031 (Ext. 250)
Fax: 82-2-732-2037

Copyright 2013 Darakwon, Inc.

All rights reserved. No part of this publication may be reproduced, stored in a retrieval system, or transmitted in any form or by any means, electronic, mechanical, photocopying or otherwise, without the prior consent of the copyright owner. Refund after purchase is possible only according to the company regulations. Contact the above telephone number for any inquiries. Consumer damages caused by loss, damage, etc. can be compensated according to the consumer dispute resolution standards announced by the Korea Fair Trade Commission. An incorrectly collated book will be exchanged.

ISBN 978-89-277-0678-6 58740
978-89-277-0677-9 58740 (set)

www.darakwon.co.kr

Components Main Book / Workbook
19 18 17 16 15 14 13   24 25 26 27 28

Instilling Knowledge and Skills
for Thoughtful Debate

DEBATE Pro

Book 1

DARAKWON

Preface

The *Debate Pro* series is designed to provide students with an intermediate EFL ability with a sound understanding of a variety of debate topics and develop their speaking, listening, and critical thinking skills through debate. The series consists of eight sets of books, each of which includes a Main Book and a Workbook. Each Main Book includes five chapters covering five debate skills. Within each chapter, there are two units which each cover different topics for a total of ten debate topics per book. The Workbook supplements the Main Book by helping students understand the topic more deeply, developing skills for making examples and doing research, and evaluating the debates. The Workbook can be used in class and for homework assignments.

In the book, every debate topic is introduced with a large color photograph relating to the topic. Students are asked to analyze the picture and formulate opinions about the topic through a series of six warm-up questions. The topic is then explained in more detail through a reading passage of about 300 words which briefly presents background information about the topic before outlining arguments in favor of and against the topic. The passages are followed by vocabulary and comprehension exercises. Students are then required to apply what they have learned from the passage to answer a series of in-depth questions relating to the debate topic. Following these questions, students are given opinion examples before learning the debate skill for each topic. Finally, students will have the chance to apply their knowledge to create a full debate with the assistance of sample arguments and a debate flow chart.

Each book provides free MP3 files with recordings of the reading passages and opinion examples for every unit. There is also a Teacher's Guide available at www.darakwon.co.kr that includes answer keys and sample answers for every unit as well as teaching tips and suggestions for supplementing the material.

The *Debate Pro* series has the following features:

- Ten different debate topics per book covering a range of themes including education, technology, relationships, and responsibility
- Reading passages which provide a general understanding of arguments both for and against the given topic
- Questions that require students to formulate arguments and supporting opinions about each topic
- Five different debate skills per book designed to improve students' critical thinking and speaking skills
- Sample opinions and argument examples which help students develop their own arguments
- Free MP3 files with recordings of all passages and sample opinions

Contents

About This Book _7

Chapter 1
Defining a Motion

Unit 01 Year-Round Schools _12
Unit 02 Keeping Pets _22

Chapter 2
Manners during Debate

Unit 03 Banning Junk Food in Schools _34
Unit 04 Animal Testing _44

Chapter 3
Brainstorming

Unit 05 Beauty Pageants _56
Unit 06 Violent Video Games _66

Chapter 4
Introducing an Argument Clearly

Unit 07 Giving Children Allowances _78
Unit 08 Elementary School Uniforms _88

Chapter 5
Listing Supporting Arguments

Unit 09 English as the World Language _100
Unit 10 Social Networking Sites for Education _110

About This Book

Overview

Debate Pro main book consists of five chapters. Each chapter contains two units with each focusing on the same debate skill. Every unit is further subdivided into part A and part B. Part A, Learning about the Topic, introduces students to the topic of the unit and consists of approximately one hour of learning material. Part B, Debating the Topic, requires students to formulate their arguments and debate the topic of the unit. The total time required for Part B is also approximately one hour.

Introduction for each section

Warm-up

This part includes a picture related to the topic for students to analyze. The pictures are followed by six warm-up questions. The questions in Part A require students to analyze the picture and can be answered as a class. In Part B, students draw upon their knowledge about the topic to answer questions with a partner.

Reading Passage

This part consists of a single reading passage approximately 300 words in length. The passage introduces general background information about the topic and presents specific arguments with examples both in favor of and against the topic.

Vocabulary Check

Each reading passage is followed by five vocabulary questions to bolster students' vocabulary and ensure their understanding of the passage.

Comprehension Questions

Each reading passage includes four paired-choice reading comprehension questions. The questions ask students about the main idea of passage, factual information, and reasoning from the passage.

Questions for Debate

This portion consists of five open-ended questions related to the topic. The students must formulate opinions about each question and give reasons for their opinions. Key phrases are provided to help students improve their speaking skills.

Opinion Examples

In this section, two opinion examples for and against the topic are provided. Students are required to understand the main idea of each example opinion and its supporting arguments. They must also provide an additional argument for each opinion.

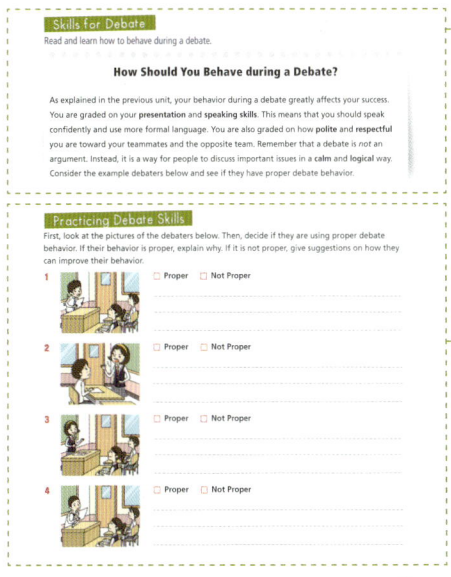

Skills for Debate

This section introduces a debate skill and explains key concepts related to the topic. Each chapter focuses on a single debate skill across two units.

Practicing Debate Skills

This exercise follows each debate skill explanation to ensure that students understand the skill and can use it during their debate.

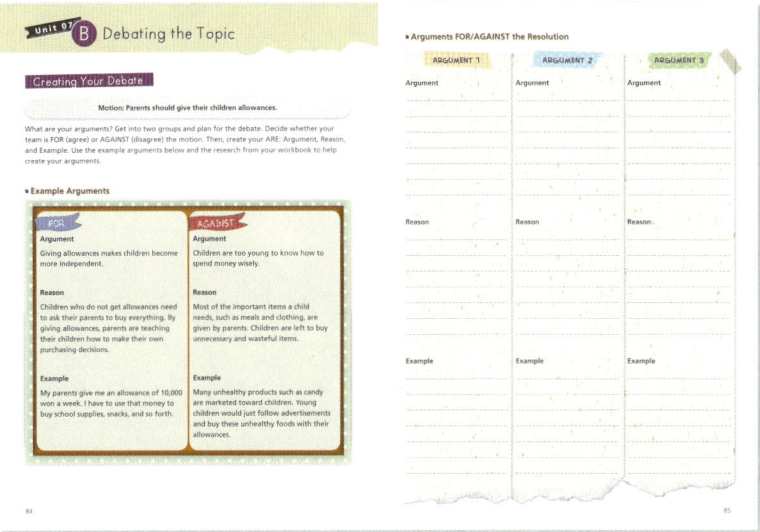

Creating Your Debate

This section begins by introducing the skills of ARE: Argument, Reason, and Example. Following this are two sample arguments, one for PRO and one for CON, with sample notes for the ARE. On the next page are three blank columns for students to work in teams and create their AREs.

Actual Debate

This portion consists of a debate flow chart. The chart outlines the order of debate and provides sample phrases to help students use proper debate language.

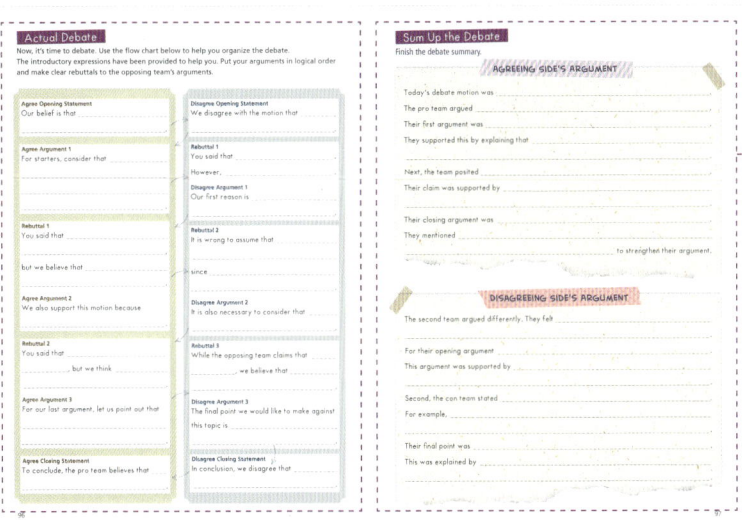

Sum Up the Debate

The final section requires students to summarize the arguments presented by both the PRO and CON teams during the debate. Sample phrases are given to help students.

Chapter 1

Defining a Motion

Unit 01 Year-Round Schools

Unit 02 Keeping Pets

Unit 01: Year-Round Schools

WARM-UP

A. Discuss the following questions as a class.
1. What do you see in the pictures above?
2. Which is more important: having fun or studying? Why?
3. How do you think these two pictures relate to the topic?

B. Answer the following questions with a partner.
1. Do you think you can learn more by going to school throughout the year?
2. Why do you think schools created long summer vacations in the first place?
3. What are the main benefits of summer vacations for students? For teachers?

Unit 01 A Learning about the Topic

Should students be required to go to school throughout the year?

Read the passage and underline the main ideas. Track 01

For generations, students have had a three-month-long vacation in the summer. The purpose of this was so that children could work on their parents' farms. However, most people today do not live on farms. In response, educators have created year-round schools. Instead of having one long break in the summer, year-round schools have several breaks throughout the year. The total number of days students spend in school is usually the same. **Backers** of year-round schools argue that they are beneficial for students, but is this really the case?

The main argument in favor of year-round schools is that students learn more. During the long summer break, students forget a lot of what they learned in the **prior** school year. This means that teachers start each school year reviewing material from the year before. This wastes time. Similarly, year-round schools can **enhance** student achievement. Students who study throughout the year are more likely to remember the material they learned. This helps them have higher test scores. Year-round schools especially benefit at-risk students, who are the students that are likely to quit school. Year-round schools keep these students busy during the summer. Otherwise, they may get into trouble.

Not everybody is in favor of year-round schools. One such group is the teachers themselves. Many teachers spend the summer receiving additional training, which helps them become better teachers. The students may also suffer. Younger students spend the summer vacation playing with their friends and traveling. These are important for their **cognitive** and social development. Older students are also busy during the summer vacation. They play sports, work at part-time jobs, and prepare their college applications. There are also economic issues to consider. Older schools were not built to be used during the summer. They do not have air conditioning or good ventilation. To allow year-round schooling, these schools would have to **renovate** their facilities. This would be very expensive.

Vocabulary Check

Choose the correct word for each definition.

| cognitive | backer | prior | enhance | renovate |

1 to rebuild or remodel   _____
2 to increase or improve   _____
3 a person who agrees with an idea _____
4 relating to the mind   _____
5 from a time before   _____

Comprehension Questions

Check the correct answer for each question.

1 What was the original reason that schools had summer vacation?
   ☐ To allow students to work on farms
   ☐ To give students enough time to rest

2 What do teachers usually do at the beginning of the school year?
   ☐ They go over the material from the previous year.
   ☐ They help students prepare for their tests.

3 Which group of students benefits the most from year-round schools?
   ☐ students with high test scores
   ☐ students who are at risk

4 Why are some teachers not in favor of year-round schools?
   ☐ Because they want to take summer vacations
   ☐ Because they want to receive additional training during the summer

Questions for Debate

Think of and share ideas to explore the debatable issues in the article. Be sure to state your opinion clearly and to provide one supporting idea for each opinion.

1. Would you rather go to a school with a traditional calendar or a year-round school?

   I would rather _____

   _____.

   The reason I feel this way is _____

   _____.

2. Do you believe year-round schools help children learn more? Why or why not?

   To me, it seems that _____

   _____.

   The reason is that _____

   _____.

3. Which types of students would benefit the most from year-round schools?

   I think that _____

   _____.

   I believe this because _____

   _____.

4. How would year-round schooling affect teachers?

   It is my belief that _____

   _____.

   For example, _____

   _____.

5. Why do you think some parents do not want to send their children to year-round schools?

   I feel that _____

   _____.

   To make myself clear, let me say that _____

   _____.

Opinion Examples

Look at the opinion examples about the motion below and answer the questions.

Motion: All schools should adopt the year-round calendar.

Opinion A Track 02

I believe that schools should keep the traditional calendar. Students have had summer vacations for several centuries. This system works well, so there is no reason to change it. Students also need a chance to get away from school. They need to be able to relax, spend time with their families, and have fun. This is what my family does. Every summer, we take special trips to various places. Last year, we traveled to Florida and stayed there for an entire month. If summer vacations are taken away, we can't do this anymore.

Opinion B Track 03

It's time for schools to change to the year-round calendar. The traditional school calendar was made so that students could help on their families' farms. Of course, almost nobody lives on a farm anymore, so that is no longer important. Year-round schools help students learn more and remember better. I know that during each summer, I forget some of the concepts we learned in school the year before. The teachers know this too, because they start each year by reviewing last year's material. With year-round schools, I could focus better on my schoolwork and still get the breaks I need.

1 Underline the main idea of each opinion.

2 Which opinion is for the topic? Which one is against it?
- FOR: _____
- AGAINST: _____

3 What supporting ideas does each opinion give?
- Opinion A: _____
- Opinion B: _____

4 Create one more supporting idea for each argument.
- Opinion A: _____
- Opinion B: _____

Skills for Debate

Read and learn how to create a motion.

How Can You Create a Motion?

In order to have a debate, there must be a **motion** first. The motion is essentially the topic of a debate. A **strong motion** must be **clear** and **easy to understand**. It must also be **debatable**. In other words, there must be strong arguments both FOR and AGAINST the topic. On the other hand, a **weak motion** simply lists a **fact**, makes a **generalization**, or is **too broad**. To debate well, you must first learn how to create a strong, clear motion.

Practicing Debate Skills

Read each of the sample motions below. Then, decide if they are strong or weak. If they are strong, explain why. If they are weak, rewrite them to make them stronger.

1. All teachers should earn more money. (☐ STRONG   ☐ WEAK)
   → _____

2. Summer is the best season of the year. (☐ STRONG   ☐ WEAK)
   → _____

3. Parents have the right to physically punish their children. (☐ STRONG   ☐ WEAK)
   → _____

4. Ice cream is high in fat and calories. (☐ STRONG   ☐ WEAK)
   → _____

Unit 01 B Debating the Topic

Creating Your Debate

Motion: All schools should adopt the year-round calendar.

What are your arguments? Get into two groups and plan for the debate. Decide whether your team is FOR (agree) or AGAINST (disagree) the motion. Then, create your ARE: Argument, Reason, and Example. Use the example arguments below and the research from your workbook to help create your arguments.

■ **Example Arguments**

FOR

Argument

Year-round schools enhance students' academic achievements.

Reason

Students have shorter breaks between semesters. As a result, students are less likely to forget the material they covered in the previous term.

Example

Studies show that students at year-round schools have higher test scores on average. One study found that their math scores are almost 2.5 points higher.

AGAINST

Argument

Students suffer cognitively and socially because of year-round schools.

Reason

Students need to have enough time to rest and to be away from school. Fun and unstructured activities help them learn and grow.

Example

Dr. Kenneth R. Ginsburg published a study showing that playing and having fun help children concentrate more on schoolwork.

Arguments FOR/AGAINST the Motion

ARGUMENT 1

Argument

Reason

Example

ARGUMENT 2

Argument

Reason

Example

ARGUMENT 3

Argument

Reason

Example

Actual Debate

Now, it's time to debate. Use the flow chart below to help you organize the debate.
The introductory expressions have been provided to help you. Put your arguments in logical order and make clear rebuttals to the opposing team's arguments.

Agree Opening Statement
We, the members of the pro team, feel that _____.

Disagree Opening Statement
It is our opinion that _____ should be banned.

Agree Argument 1
Our first argument in favor of the topic is _____.

Rebuttal 1
The pro team claims that _____.
However, _____.

Disagree Argument 1
One problem caused by _____ is _____.

Rebuttal 1
You said that _____, but we believe that _____.

Agree Argument 2
We also support this motion because _____.

Rebuttal 2
Your argument that _____ is incorrect.

Disagree Argument 2
Furthermore, consider the drawbacks of _____.

Rebuttal 2
Our team disagrees that _____.

Agree Argument 3
Finally, we feel _____ is true because _____.

Rebuttal 3
In spite of your argument that _____, we believe that _____.

Disagree Argument 3
The final point we would like to make against this topic is _____.

Agree Closing Statement
Overall, we agree that _____.

Disagree Closing Statement
In conclusion, we disagree that _____.

Sum Up the Debate

Finish the debate summary.

AGREEING SIDE'S ARGUMENT

The topic of today's debate was _____.

The first team completely _____.

Their first argument was _____.

They supported this by explaining that _____

_____.

For their second argument, they presented _____.

For instance, _____

_____.

Finally, they reasoned _____.

For example, _____

_____.

DISAGREEING SIDE'S ARGUMENT

The second team argued differently. They felt _____

_____.

They started by arguing that _____.

To support this, they explained _____

_____.

Their next argument was _____.

For example, _____

_____.

To conclude, they contended _____.

Specifically, they mentioned _____

_____.

Unit 02 Keeping Pets

A. Discuss the following questions as a class.
1. What do you see in the picture above?
2. How do you think the woman feels? What about the dog?
3. Do you think animals are happy living as people's pets?

B. Answer the following questions with a partner.
1. Why do you think human beings first began raising animals as pets?
2. Do you think having pets can make people healthier?
3. What are some of the potential dangers of keeping animals as pets?

Unit 02   A Learning about the Topic

Should people be allowed to keep animals as pets?

Read the passage and underline the main ideas.

 Track 04

It is often said that dogs are man's best friend. People say this for a good reason. Human beings and dogs have hunted and lived together for thousands of years. Unsurprisingly, there is **ample** evidence that keeping pets provides numerous benefits. Even so, having pets can result in problems for the humans that keep them and the animals themselves. Perhaps it is time for humans to set their animal friends free once and for all.

There are many advantages to keeping pets. For one, pets provide **companionship**. Most pet owners give their pets names and treat them as family members. They enjoy feeding, grooming, and playing with their pets. Keeping pets is also a great way to teach children responsibility. Children have to look after their pets regularly. They have to give their pets food and water and make sure they get enough exercise. Evidence also suggests that having pets is good for your health. In one study, 55 percent of **respondents** claimed that having a pet lowers their stress. Another study found that pet owners were 40 percent less likely to suffer from a serious heart attack than non-pet owners.

However, not everything about keeping pets is beneficial. One problem is that owners do not always look after their pets properly. In today's busy world, people sometimes do not have enough time to give their animals the attention that they need. Owners may not feed their pets often enough. Some pets, especially dogs, need lots of exercise. There is also the issue of **breeding** pets. In many cases, animals bred as pets do not get adopted as pets. Rather than being able to live their lives, these animals are **put to sleep**. Pets can also pose a danger to their owners. Many animals can pass diseases to their human owners, and, in some cases, dogs have reportedly attacked their owners.

Vocabulary Check

Choose the correct word for each definition.

| ample | companionship | respondent | breed | put to sleep |

1 to keep animals to have more of them _____
2 to end an animal's life _____
3 the feeling that comes with having friends _____
4 a person who participates in a survey _____
5 more than enough; plenty _____

Comprehension Questions

Check the correct answer for each question.

1 What was the original reason that human beings raised animals?
  ☐ To help with hunting
  ☐ To help raise children

2 What are some ways that people treat their pets as family members according to the passage?
  ☐ They care for their pets and play with them.
  ☐ They take their pets to the doctor and exercise with them.

3 Which is a health benefit that is provided by pets?
  ☐ Being less likely to feel tired
  ☐ Having a lower risk for a heart attack

4 Why do some people not give their pets enough attention?
  ☐ Because they are busy and do not have enough time
  ☐ Because they decide they do not like their pets anymore

Questions for Debate

Think of and share ideas to explore the debatable issues in the article. Be sure to state your opinion clearly and to provide one supporting idea for each opinion.

1 What are some ways that pets can help their owners?

In my opinion, _____

_____.

For example, _____

_____.

2 Do you think that having pets helps people become healthier? Why or why not?

I think that _____

_____.

The reason is that _____

_____.

3 Who benefits more from keeping pets, the owners or the animals?

From my perspective, it seems that _____

_____.

The reason I believe this is _____

_____.

4 How does raising animals as pets lead to problems concerning animal overpopulation?

It can cause _____

_____.

This is due to the fact that _____

_____.

5 What are some reasons that people would prefer not to keep pets?

Some possible reasons are _____

_____.

Allow me to illustrate this by mentioning _____

_____.

Opinion Examples

Look at the opinion examples about the motion below and answer the questions.

Motion: People should be allowed to keep animals as pets.

Opinion A Track 05

Having pets may seem like a good idea. However, there are several drawbacks that must be considered. Pets may help their owners relieve their stress, but what about the pets themselves? Imagine being trapped in a small house all day. Would you be happy? Of course not. But when pet owners are too busy to care for their animals, this is what often happens. Then, there is the issue of overpopulation. Each year, millions of animals are put to sleep. The reason is simply that no one wants them as pets. These animals are born into the world only to be taken out of it.

Opinion B Track 06

I can't imagine living without my dog Buddy. Keeping pets is great for both people and animals. When animals are kept as pets, they often receive great treatment. Although some pet owners may not take care of their pets, most owners feed, wash, and play with their pets all the time. Pets also provide real companionship for people, especially people without any other family nearby. Moreover, many pet owners work hard to prevent pet overpopulation. They do this by reducing the number of animals that are born so that too many animals do not have to be put to sleep.

1. Underline the main idea of each opinion.

2. Which opinion is for the topic? Which one is against it?
   - FOR: _____
   - AGAINST: _____

3. What supporting ideas does each opinion give?
   - Opinion A: _____
   - Opinion B: _____

4. Create one more supporting idea for each argument.
   - Opinion A: _____
   - Opinion B: _____

Skills for Debate

Read and learn how to create a motion.

How Can You Create a Motion?

Now that you know how to create a strong motion, you need to learn how to **define** your motion. Before the debate, the pro team should define the **exact meaning** of the motion. This can be done by clearly defining the **key words** in the motion. You may use a dictionary to help you define these words. The way the pro team defines the motion can change the entire direction of the debate, so be sure to get the wording right!

Practicing Debate Skills

First, find and underline the key words in the motions below. Then, define each key word with a definition that can clarify the meaning of the debate. An example is given for you.

1 <u>Violent</u> <u>video games</u> should be <u>banned</u>.
   ① **violent:** showing dangerous or destructive behavior
   ② **video games:** games played on consoles or computers that use computer graphics
   ③ **ban:** to forbid or disallow people from using something

2 Children should be required to do household chores.
   ① _____ : _____
   ② _____ : _____
   ③ _____ : _____

3 Teachers must assign homework to their students every day.
   ① _____ : _____
   ② _____ : _____
   ③ _____ : _____

4 Life exists on Mars.
   ① _____ : _____
   ② _____ : _____
   ③ _____ : _____

Unit 02 B Debating the Topic

Creating Your Debate

Motion: People should be allowed to keep animals as pets.

What are your arguments? Get into two groups and plan for the debate. Decide whether your team is FOR (agree) or AGAINST (disagree) the motion. Then, create your ARE: Argument, Reason, and Example. Use the example arguments below and the research from your workbook to help create your arguments.

■ Example Arguments

FOR

Argument

Keeping pets helps people stay healthier.

Reason

Pets make people feel happier and less stressed. This can reduce people's blood pressure and reduce feelings of depression, allowing people to be healthier.

Example

Research shows that spending time with pets causes your body to go through physical changes. Your body produces less cortisol, a stress hormone. At the same time, it makes more serotonin, which is associated with well-being.

AGAINST

Argument

Keeping animals as pets is harmful to the animals themselves.

Reason

Many pet owners simply do not have enough time or energy to properly care for their pets. As a result, many pets live in inadequate conditions. In extreme cases, the pets are abandoned.

Example

According to recent statistics, over four million dogs are abandoned in the U.S. each year. Many of these dogs are sent to animal shelters where they are put to sleep.

Arguments FOR/AGAINST the Motion

ARGUMENT 1

Argument

Reason

Example

ARGUMENT 2

Argument

Reason

Example

ARGUMENT 3

Argument

Reason

Example

Actual Debate

Now, it's time to debate. Use the flow chart below to help you organize the debate. The introductory expressions have been provided to help you. Put your arguments in logical order and make clear rebuttals to the opposing team's arguments.

Agree Opening Statement
It is our belief that _____ _____ is beneficial.

Disagree Opening Statement
We contend that _____ _____ has several drawbacks.

Agree Argument 1
For our first argument, we believe _____ _____ _____ _____ _____.

Rebuttal 1
Our opponents believe that _____ _____
Even so, _____.

Disagree Argument 1
The primary shortcoming of _____ is _____.

Rebuttal 1
Your team argued that _____ _____, yet we feel that _____.

Rebuttal 2
Your statement that _____ _____ is not true. _____.

Agree Argument 2
Second, it is undeniable that _____ _____ _____.

Disagree Argument 2
Next, let us point out that _____ _____.

Rebuttal 2
Even though _____, we must point out that _____ _____.

Rebuttal 3
Our team refutes the idea that _____ _____ _____.

Agree Argument 3
Our final argument is _____ _____ _____.

Disagree Argument 3
The last factor to consider is _____ _____.

Agree Closing Statement
We, the members of the pro team, feel that _____ _____ _____.

Disagree Closing Statement
To sum up, it is the con team's belief that _____ _____ _____.

Sum Up the Debate

Finish the debate summary.

AGREEING SIDE'S ARGUMENT

The topic of today's debate was _____.

The first team contended _____.

For their opening argument, they explained _____.

The example they gave was _____
_____.

Their second argument was _____.

To be specific, _____
_____.

The team concluded by arguing _____.

For instance, _____
_____.

DISAGREEING SIDE'S ARGUMENT

In contrast, the second team argued _____
_____.

First, they stated that _____.

This argument was supported by _____
_____.

Their second argument was _____.

To go into detail, _____
_____.

For their closing argument, they explained _____.

Specifically, they stated _____
_____.

Chapter 2

Manners during Debate

Unit 03 Banning Junk Food in Schools

Unit 04 Animal Testing

Unit 03 — Banning Junk Food in Schools

A. Discuss the following questions as a class.

1. What do you see in the picture above?
2. How do you think the girl in the picture feels about eating her meal?
3. How often do you think children should be allowed to eat junk food?

B. Answer the following questions with a partner.

1. In your opinion, are the lunches at your school healthy?
2. What are some advantages of offering junk food in schools?
3. Why do you think schools allow junk food to be sold in the first place?

Unit 03   A Learning about the Topic

Should schools get rid of junk food from their lunchrooms?

Read the passage and underline the main ideas.

Recent studies have found that nearly 20 percent of American elementary school children are overweight. This number continues to rise. There are many potential causes of this problem. One of the most likely is the sale of junk food in schools. Across the nation, many schools have vending machines full of candy bars and potato chips. Oftentimes, these schools also serve pizza, fried chicken, and other unhealthy foods to their students. Still, there are many who believe that junk food is not responsible for the rise in childhood **obesity**. Should junk food be allowed to stay in our schools?

Those in favor of banning junk food in schools argue there is a clear **link** between junk food and childhood obesity. One of the most common supporting arguments is that childhood is the time of learning about eating habits. When schools serve unhealthy foods, children begin to believe that eating junk food is acceptable or even normal. Another popular argument deals with government responsibility. Most schools are public, which means that they are run by the government. Supporters of the junk food ban argue that it is the role of the government to solve the nation's problems. Therefore, the government should ban junk food in schools to **prevent** future generations from becoming overweight.

Even so, not all are **convinced** that removing junk food from schools is the answer. Opponents argue that schools teach their students about making choices. This can be done by offering a variety of foods, both healthy and unhealthy. By removing junk food from schools, students are denied this learning opportunity. Moreover, eating habits alone do not cause obesity. Exercise is also necessary to prevent weight gain. It is for this reason that schools should **encourage** their students to do more physical activities. This can be done by having more gym classes or offering more sports programs.

Vocabulary Check

Choose the correct word for each definition.

| obesity | link | prevent | convinced | encourage |

1 to make someone more likely to do something _____
2 to stop something from happening _____
3 a connection between ideas _____
4 the state of being very overweight _____
5 believing something to be true _____

Comprehension Questions

Check the correct answer for each question.

1 What do some people believe is causing the rise in childhood obesity?
   - ☐ The sale of junk food in schools
   - ☐ The reduction in the number of physical education classes

2 How does serving junk food in schools affect children's eating habits?
   - ☐ It causes children's bodies to become used to unhealthy foods.
   - ☐ It teaches children that eating junk food is acceptable and normal.

3 How can schools help students prevent weight gain?
   - ☐ By offering more gym classes
   - ☐ By offering nutritional education

4 What educational benefit does junk food offer students?
   - ☐ It shows students how junk foods are made.
   - ☐ It teaches them about making healthy eating choices.

Questions for Debate

Think of and share ideas to explore the debatable issues in the article. Be sure to state your opinion clearly and to provide one supporting idea for each opinion.

1 Do you think schools should be responsible for the eating habits of their students?

In my opinion, _____
_____.

The reason is _____
_____.

2 Should schools be allowed to control what foods their students are allowed to eat at school?

I believe that _____
_____.

For example, _____
_____.

3 Is allowing junk food in schools the main cause of student obesity?

My feeling is _____
_____.

To be more specific, _____
_____.

4 Do you think students would choose healthy eating options if they were offered along with junk foods?

To me, it seems that _____
_____.

This is my opinion because _____
_____.

5 Who is more to blame for the rise of junk foods in schools, food companies or the schools themselves?

From my perspective, it is obvious that _____
_____.

My reasoning is that _____
_____.

Opinion Examples

Look at the opinion examples about the motion below and answer the questions.

> Motion: Schools should ban junk food from their lunchrooms.

Opinion A Track 08

Banning junk food is not the answer to solving student obesity. Sure, students eat unhealthy foods in school, but they don't usually eat too much of them. For example, my school only serves students one piece of pizza for lunch. This has about 300 calories. This amount of junk food alone cannot cause obesity. The bigger problem is that schools are getting rid of their physical education classes. Most students spend their time outside school studying, playing video games, or surfing the Internet. So schools should add more P.E. classes. That would help students burn more calories and lose weight.

Opinion B Track 09

As more children become obese, it is clear that schools must find ways to solve the problem. One of the easiest solutions is to remove junk food from their cafeterias. The truth is that foods like potato chips and candy bars have no place in our schools. They have almost no vitamins. They are made from processed ingredients. They are high in fat and calories. Rather than teaching students that eating junk food is okay, schools should promote healthy eating habits. One way they could do this is by serving only healthy foods. Another way is to offer nutrition classes.

1. Underline the main idea of each opinion.

2. Which opinion is for the topic? Which one is against it?
   - FOR: _____
   - AGAINST: _____

3. What supporting ideas does each opinion give?
   - Opinion A: _____
   - Opinion B: _____

4. Create one more supporting idea for each argument.
   - Opinion A: _____
   - Opinion B: _____

Skills for Debate

Read and learn how to behave during a debate.

How Should You Behave During a Debate?

Your **behavior** during a debate is important for successfully delivering your **arguments** and **reasons**. In general, you should **stand up straight**, **look at your audience**, and **speak with confidence**. You should also remember to **be polite** and **respectful** to your teammates as well as the judges and opposing team. Part of being a winning debater is correcting your bad habits and **developing good debate behavior**.

Practicing Debate Skills

Read the list of behaviors below. Then, decide whether they are APPROPRIATE or INAPPROPRIATE debate behavior.

1. Leaning against the desk while you speak
2. Scratching your head as you talk
3. Stressing the positives of your ideas
4. Insulting the other team's members
5. Pointing out the mistakes in the other team's ideas
6. Speaking with an even tone of voice
7. Arguing with the debate judge
8. Looking at others while you speak
9. Only looking at your notes while you talk
10. Using words such as "sir," "ma'am," "please," and "thank you"

APPROPRIATE Behavior

INAPPROPRIATE Behavior

Unit 03 B Debating the Topic

Creating Your Debate

Motion: Schools should ban junk food from their lunchrooms.

What are your arguments? Get into two groups and plan for the debate. Decide whether your team is FOR (agree) or AGAINST (disagree) the motion. Then, create your ARE: Argument, Reason, and Example. Use the example arguments below and the research from your workbook to help create your arguments.

- **Example Arguments**

FOR

Argument

When schools serve junk food, children learn that eating unhealthy food is acceptable.

Reason

Young children are still learning about the world around them and are, therefore, easily influenced by it. Serving junk food in schools encourages young people to eat it.

Example

A study by the National Bureau of Economic Research found that every 10-percent increase in the number of schools that serve junk food raises the average body mass index (BMI) of all students by 1 point.

AGAINST

Argument

Students are given the opportunity to learn about healthy eating habits when junk food is served in schools.

Reason

Young children are still learning about the world, both the good and the bad. Exposing children to junk food lets them learn how it affects the body firsthand. This is an important life lesson.

Example

Most middle and high schools offer many different lunch choices for students, including healthy and less healthy foods. Students can choose for themselves to eat pizza every day or to get more fruits and vegetables.

Arguments FOR/AGAINST the Motion

ARGUMENT 1

Argument

Reason

Example

ARGUMENT 2

Argument

Reason

Example

ARGUMENT 3

Argument

Reason

Example

Actual Debate

Now, it's time to debate. Use the flow chart below to help you organize the debate.
The introductory expressions have been provided to help you. Put your arguments in logical order and make clear rebuttals to the opposing team's arguments.

Agree Opening Statement
Our opinion is that _____
_____
_____ should be banned.

Agree Argument 1
For starters, consider that _____
_____
_____
_____
_____.

Rebuttal 1
Your team claims that _____
_____,
but we believe that _____
_____
_____.

Agree Argument 2
Second, it is undeniable that _____
_____
_____.

Rebuttal 2
Our opponents have made the argument that _____
_____.

Agree Argument 3
Our last argument is _____
_____
_____
_____.

Agree Closing Statement
To conclude, our team feels that _____
_____
_____.

Disagree Opening Statement
The advantages of _____
_____
_____ outweigh the drawbacks.

Rebuttal 1
Our opponents feel that _____
_____
_____.
However, _____
_____.

Disagree Argument 1
First, it must be pointed out that _____
_____
_____.

Rebuttal 2
Your argument that _____
_____
_____,
yet _____.

Disagree Argument 2
The next idea we would like you to think about is _____.
_____

Rebuttal 3
The opposing team incorrectly believes that _____
_____.

Disagree Argument 3
Finally, it should be mentioned that _____
_____
_____.

Disagree Closing Statement
Our overall opinion is that _____
_____
_____.

Sum Up the Debate

Finish the debate summary.

AGREEING SIDE'S ARGUMENT

Our debate topic today was _____.

The pro side's main argument was _____.

Their first supporting idea was _____.

For their example, they mentioned _____
_____.

Next, they explained _____.

In more detail, _____
_____.

For their final point, the pro team argued _____.

Specifically, _____
_____.

DISAGREEING SIDE'S ARGUMENT

The con side presented the opposite opinion. They stated _____
_____.

Their opening argument was _____.

Their supporting idea was _____
_____.

Second, they explained _____.

To share their example, _____
_____.

For their final argument, the con team mentioned _____.

For their example, they said _____
_____.

Unit 04 Animal Testing

A. Discuss the following questions as a class.
1. What do you see in the picture above?
2. What do you think the researcher is injecting into the animal?
3. How does the animal look in this situation?

B. Answer the following questions with a partner.
1. Do you believe studying animals helps scientists develop better medicines?
2. Do you think animals have a right to live without pain and suffering?
3. What are some situations in which it is okay to test animals? Not okay?

Unit 04 A Learning about the Topic

Should animals be used in scientific experiments?

Read the passage and underline the main ideas.

 Track 10

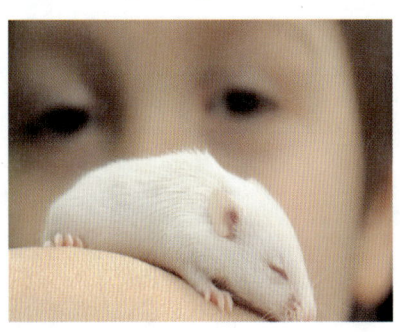

Animal testing is the use of nonhuman creatures in scientific experiments. Tests include studying animal behavior and creating new medicines. It is estimated that between 50 and 100 million animals are tested on each year. Some of the animals most commonly used in tests are mice, rabbits, and chimpanzees. Animal testing is a highly **controversial** issue, and there are strong arguments both for and against it.

Many large organizations support animal testing. They support it because the results of animal testing are often very useful. Animals used in tests and human beings are genetically similar. Mice share 99 percent of their genes with human beings, and chimpanzees share an even greater 99.4 percent. These animals also have very similar organ and nervous systems as human beings. This means that a drug will affect humans in the same way it affects the animals. Furthermore, the use of animal experimentation has **led to** the creation of many important medical treatments. Some treatments made using animal testing include those for Alzheimer's disease, Parkinson's disease, and autism. By using animals in experiments, **breakthrough** treatments become possible.

In spite of these benefits, animal testing has many **critics**. The most common criticism is that animals have a right not to be harmed. It is true that animals used in tests are genetically and physically similar to human beings. This means they must experience pain during animal testing. Researchers often cover these animals in chemicals that cause blindness. They sometimes give the animals drugs that can kill them. Even if the animals survive the testing experiments, they are usually killed afterward anyway. This is clearly a **violation** of the animals' rights. Instead of animal testing, critics suggest using alternative testing methods. Some of these include using human cell cultures, creating computer models, and studying human volunteers. With so many alternatives, it seems that animal testing is no longer necessary.

Vocabulary Check

Choose the correct word for each definition.

> controversial   lead to   breakthrough   critic   violation

1 to guide someone toward something _____
2 a person who disagrees with and attacks an idea _____
3 the act of ignoring a person's or animal's rights _____
4 an important discovery that occurs after a lot of study _____
5 causing much discussion or argument _____

Comprehension Questions

Check the correct answer for each question.

1 What is one reason that animals are used in scientific experiments?
 □ To create safer food ingredients
 □ To develop new medical drugs

2 Why are the results of animal tests often very useful?
 □ Because animals and human beings are genetically similar
 □ Because animals suffer from the same illnesses as human beings

3 Which diseases have had treatments developed through animal testing? Choose TWO correct answers.
 □ Parkinson's disease   □ cancer
 □ Alpers' disease   □ autism

4 What solution do critics have for animal testing?
 □ Using alternative testing methods such as computer models
 □ Allowing the animals to live after the completion of an experiment

Questions for Debate

Think of and share ideas to explore the debatable issues in the article. Be sure to state your opinion clearly and to provide one supporting idea for each opinion.

1 People raise animals for food. Is animal testing different? Why or why not?

I believe that _____

_____.

The reason I feel this way is _____

_____.

2 Do you think that animals feel pain in the same ways that humans do? Why or why not?

It is my opinion that _____

_____.

The reason is _____

_____.

3 Does the fact that animal testing ends human suffering make it more or less justifiable?

From my perspective, it seems that _____

_____.

I believe this because _____

_____.

4 In what ways do you think animals benefit from animal testing?

It is my belief that _____

_____.

For instance, _____

_____.

5 What alternative forms of testing do you think can be as effective as animal testing?

I feel that _____

_____.

To give you an idea, consider that _____

_____.

Opinion Examples

Look at the opinion examples about the motion below and answer the questions.

Motion: Animal testing is necessary for scientific and medical developments to continue.

Opinion A Track 11

Animal testing sounds cruel, but it is necessary to allow science to develop fully. Nearly all important medicines, chemicals, and cosmetics were created through animal testing. Testing with animals is the best way for scientists to be sure of the safety of their products. The truth is that using other forms of testing such as computer models is not as accurate as using living animals. Without accurate tests, human beings are more likely to get hurt or even die from these newly developed products and treatments. Besides, animal testing can benefit the animals themselves. The animals can live better through the creation of new animal medicines and more nutritious foods.

Opinion B Track 12

Animal testing has gone on long enough. Animal testing is a violation of animals' rights. Animals don't have voices and can't agree to animal testing, not that they'd want to. Most animal tests involve dangerous chemicals that can eat the animals' skin. Other times, animals have computers attached directly to their brains. That doesn't sound enjoyable at all. You might also think that all animal tests are for breakthrough medical treatments. But a lot of the time, new cosmetics such as makeup and perfume are tested on animals. These tests are unnecessary and completely selfish. Let's end animal testing before it's too late.

1 Underline the main idea of each opinion.

2 Which opinion is for the topic? Which one is against it?
- FOR: _____
- AGAINST: _____

3 What supporting ideas does each opinion give?
- Opinion A: _____
- Opinion B: _____

4 Create one more supporting idea for each argument.
- Opinion A: _____
- Opinion B: _____

Skills for Debate

Read and learn how to behave during a debate.

How Should You Behave during a Debate?

As explained in the previous unit, your behavior during a debate greatly affects your success. You are graded on your **presentation** and **speaking skills**. This means that you should speak confidently and use more formal language. You are also graded on how **polite** and **respectful** you are toward your teammates and the opposite team. Remember that a debate is *not* an argument. Instead, it is a way for people to discuss important issues in a **calm** and **logical** way. Consider the example debaters below and see if they have proper debate behavior.

Practicing Debate Skills

First, look at the pictures of the debaters below. Then, decide if they are using proper debate behavior. If their behavior is proper, explain why. If it is not proper, give suggestions on how they can improve their behavior.

1 ☐ **Proper**   ☐ **Not Proper**

_____
_____
_____

2 ☐ **Proper**   ☐ **Not Proper**

_____
_____
_____

3 ☐ **Proper**   ☐ **Not Proper**

_____
_____
_____

4 ☐ **Proper**   ☐ **Not Proper**

_____
_____
_____

Unit 04 B Debating the Topic

Creating Your Debate

Motion: Animal testing is necessary for scientific and medical developments to continue.

What are your arguments? Get into two groups and plan for the debate. Decide whether your team is FOR (agree) or AGAINST (disagree) the motion. Then, create your ARE: Argument, Reason, and Example. Use the example arguments below and the research from your workbook to help create your arguments.

■ Example Arguments

FOR

Argument

Animal testing ensures that new treatments and medicines are safe and effective.

Reason

Scientists can observe the physical reactions of a new drug or chemical on a living creature. Since animals used in testing are genetically similar to humans, the results are usually accurate.

Example

One group of researchers reported that animals make good test subjects because they suffer many of the same diseases as human beings.

AGAINST

Argument

People do not have the right to make animals suffer.

Reason

Human beings force animals to participate in animal experiments despite knowing that the experiments are dangerous and painful.

Example

As human beings, we possess free will and a conscious. We know that making other creatures suffer is wrong. Therefore, we should not subject animals to cruel treatment in these tests.

Arguments FOR/AGAINST the Motion

ARGUMENT 1	ARGUMENT 2	ARGUMENT 3
Argument	**Argument**	**Argument**
Reason	**Reason**	**Reason**
Example	**Example**	**Example**

Actual Debate

Now, it's time to debate. Use the flow chart below to help you organize the debate. The introductory expressions have been provided to help you. Put your arguments in logical order and make clear rebuttals to the opposing team's arguments.

Agree Opening Statement
It is the opinion of the pro side that _____
_____
_____ .

Agree Argument 1
For our opening argument, _____
_____
_____
_____
_____ .

Rebuttal 1
The opposition argued that _____ ,
but _____ .

Agree Argument 2
Our second reason in favor of the argument is _____
_____ .

Rebuttal 2
You said that _____ .
But we think _____
_____ .

Agree Argument 3
For our last argument, let us point out that _____
_____ .

Agree Closing Statement
It is the pro team's opinion that _____
_____ .

Disagree Opening Statement
We disagree with the motion that _____
_____
_____ .

Rebuttal 1
You claimed that _____
_____ .
However, _____
_____ .

Disagree Argument 1
As for our first argument, _____
_____ .

Rebuttal 2
It is wrong to assume that _____
_____ .

Disagree Argument 2
It is also necessary to consider that _____
_____ .

Rebuttal 3
Your third argument is flawed because _____
_____
_____ .

Disagree Argument 3
Our final reason is that _____
_____ .

Disagree Closing Statement
In brief, we disagree that _____
_____ .

Sum Up the Debate

Finish the debate summary.

AGREEING SIDE'S ARGUMENT

Today's debate motion was _____.

The agree side argued _____.

For their opening argument, they claimed _____.

The example they gave was _____
_____.

Next, the team posited _____.

Their claim was supported by _____
_____.

Their final reason was _____.

In detail, _____
_____.

DISAGREEING SIDE'S ARGUMENT

In contrast, the opposition team believed _____
_____.

To start with, they claimed that _____.

They mentioned _____
_____ to support their claim.

Second, the con team stated _____.

For example, _____
_____.

Their final point was _____.

This was explained by _____
_____.

Chapter 3

Brainstorming

Unit 05 Beauty Pageants

Unit 06 Violent Video Games

Unit 05 Beauty Pageants

A. Discuss the following questions as a class.
1. What do you see in the picture above?
2. Why do you think the girl is wearing a tiara and a dress?
3. How do you think the girl feels about her appearance?

B. Answer the following questions with a partner.
1. Do you believe people should be judged based on their appearance? Why or why not?
2. What talents and abilities do you think women should have?
3. Why do you think beauty contests are still popular today?

Unit 05 A Learning about the Topic

Should beauty pageants be allowed to continue?

Read the passage and underline the main ideas.  Track 13

The first modern beauty pageant was the Miss United States beauty contest held in 1880. Since then, beauty pageants have become enormously popular. The largest pageant today is the Miss World competition. It attracts nearly three billion television viewers in 120 countries each year. Even so, these pageants have become less popular in recent years. A growing number of people feel they **objectify** women. It may finally be time for beauty pageants to end.

One of the main criticisms of beauty pageants is that they **emphasize** physical appearance. Participants in beauty contests are judged mainly on how they look. This teaches girls that they must be pretty for others to like them. They also learn that qualities such as intelligence are less important for women. This leads to a second problem: Beauty contests create unrealistic standards of beauty. Women who see beauty queens may become unhappy with their own appearance. Therefore, they may go on extreme, unhealthy diets and suffer from serious eating **disorders**. They may get plastic surgery to change their appearance. Or they may end up feeling inadequate about themselves and their bodies. This can make them depressed.

However, not everybody is against beauty pageants. Supporters of pageants claim that they focus on more than just the appearance of contestants. Most contests also have talent portions where the participants **demonstrate** their various skills. Common talents displayed are singing and dancing, but some contestants tell jokes, paint pictures, and mime. Contestants are also asked serious **intellectual** questions about society. They must explain how they can contribute to the world. Beauty pageants also create greater job opportunities for participants. Many pageant winners use their fame to become singers or actors. Others use their beauty pageant experience to start businesses and even political careers.

Vocabulary Check

Choose the correct word for each definition.

| objectify | emphasize | disorder | demonstrate | intellectual |

1 to give special attention to something _____

2 to show an example of something _____

3 to treat a person as an object _____

4 a physical condition that is not healthy _____

5 involving serious study or thought _____

Comprehension Questions

Check the correct answer for each question.

1 Why have beauty pageants become less popular in recent years?
- ☐ Because they treat women as objects
- ☐ Because there are more entertainment choices

2 What are some ways that women might respond to the contestants in beauty pageants?
- ☐ They might get plastic surgery or suffer from depression.
- ☐ They might change their diets and exercise more.

3 Why do beauty pageants focus on more than just beauty?
- ☐ Because participants must be able to solve difficult problems
- ☐ Because participants must explain how they can contribute to society

4 How do beauty pageant contestants benefit in other areas?
- ☐ They can use their experience to learn how to sing and tell jokes.
- ☐ They can use their fame to start careers in acting and politics.

Questions for Debate

Think of and share ideas to explore the debatable issues in the article. Be sure to state your opinion clearly and to provide one supporting idea for each opinion.

1 Is it wrong to appreciate a woman for her physical beauty? Why or why not?

I believe that _____
_____.

I feel this way because _____
_____.

2 In what ways are professional sports and beauty contests similar?

From my perspective, it is obvious that _____
_____.

To give an example, _____
_____.

3 Beauty pageants include a talent portion. Do you think this is necessary? Why or why not?

In my opinion, _____
_____.

The reason I feel this way is _____
_____.

4 In what ways do the contestants in beauty pageants benefit from participating in them?

I think that _____
_____.

Let me illustrate this by mentioning _____
_____.

5 In what ways does society benefit from beauty pageants?

As far as I can tell, _____
_____.

To make this clearer, allow me to say that _____
_____.

59

Opinion Examples

Look at the opinion examples about the motion below and answer the questions.

> **Motion: Beauty pageants are harmful to women and society and should be stopped.**

Opinion A Track 14

Beauty pageants may have been acceptable in the 1950s. However, they have no place in our society today. First, beauty pageants objectify women. In sports, athletes are admired for their athletic skills, which they develop through years of training. But in beauty pageants, the women are judged based only on their looks, not their skills and intelligence. And it may be true that beauty pageants include talent portions, but these are often considered less important than the beauty portions. The fact is that as long as there are beauty contests, women will be considered pretty objects first and human beings second.

Opinion B Track 15

Even though it is common to hear criticisms of beauty contests, most of them are exaggerated. Young women choose to enter beauty contests because they can develop their skills and feel good about themselves. Critics make it sound like the winners of beauty contests are always the most beautiful. However, winning a beauty contest also requires intelligence, special talents, and an outgoing personality. These are all good lessons that beauty contests teach. Like this, beauty contests give women more self-confidence. They can use their experience to become leaders in their communities. With so many benefits, it is clear that beauty contests must continue.

1 Underline the main idea of each opinion.

2 Which opinion is for the topic? Which one is against it?
- FOR: _____
- AGAINST: _____

3 What supporting ideas does each opinion give?
- Opinion A: _____
- Opinion B: _____

4 Create one more supporting idea for each argument.
- Opinion A: _____
- Opinion B: _____

Skills for Debate

Read and learn how to brainstorm in a debate.

How Can You Brainstorm Your Arguments?

Brainstorming is when you write down as many ideas about a topic as you can. When you brainstorm, you **should not worry** whether your ideas are **good** or **bad**. You simply need to **create as many ideas as you can**. For your first brainstorming session, you should focus on coming up with **supporting arguments** and deciding whether they are FOR or AGAINST the topic.

Practicing Debate Skills

Read the sample brainstorming below. Circle **F** if the idea is FOR the topic or **A** if it is AGAINST the topic. Then, brainstorm your own ideas for the second topic and decide whether they are FOR or AGAINST.

1 There should be rules against using cell phones on public transportation.

- people can become angry because of other people's cell phone conversations **(F/A)**
- people sometimes have rude or offensive conversations on their cell phones **(F/A)**
- people can use their time more efficiently if they can talk and text on their cell phones **(F/A)**

- people have the right to free speech in public **(F/A)**
- people can talk quietly on their cell phones or send messages **(F/A)**
- people have the right not to be bothered by others on public transportation **(F/A)**

2 Beauty pageants are harmful to women and society and should be stopped.

FOR	AGAINST
• _____	• _____
• _____	• _____
• _____	• _____

Unit 05 B Debating the Topic

Creating Your Debate

Motion: Beauty pageants are harmful to women and society and should be stopped.

What are your arguments? Get into two groups and plan for the debate. Decide whether your team is FOR (agree) or AGAINST (disagree) the motion. Then, create your ARE: Argument, Reason, and Example. Use the example arguments below and the research from your workbook to help create your arguments.

■ Example Arguments

FOR

Argument

Beauty contests promote an unrealistic standard of beauty.

Reason

Many participants are very thin, have perfect teeth, and have professionally done makeup and hair. Few women can ever look like the contestants in beauty contests no matter how hard they try.

Example

Sociologists argue that beauty contests put pressure on women to meet unrealistic standards of beauty. Furthermore, they promote the idea that beautiful women are "better" than other people.

AGAINST

Argument

Women should have the right to participate in beauty contests if they want to.

Reason

No one forces women to participate in beauty contests. Their participation is completely their choice, and they should not be denied this right to choose.

Example

The government allows people to participate in violent sports such as boxing. By comparison, beauty pageants are much less harmful to participants and society as a whole.

Arguments FOR/AGAINST the Motion

ARGUMENT 1	ARGUMENT 2	ARGUMENT 3
Argument	**Argument**	**Argument**
Reason	**Reason**	**Reason**
Example	**Example**	**Example**

Actual Debate

Now, it's time to debate. Use the flow chart below to help you organize the debate.
The introductory expressions have been provided to help you. Put your arguments in logical order and make clear rebuttals to the opposing team's arguments.

Agree Opening Statement
Our belief is that _____
_____
_____.

Disagree Opening Statement
We are against the idea that _____
_____
_____.

Agree Argument 1
To begin with, _____
_____
_____
_____
_____.

Rebuttal 1
You said that _____
_____,
but we feel _____
_____.

Disagree Argument 1
Our first reason is _____
_____.

Rebuttal 1
Your opinion that _____
_____ is mistaken.

Agree Argument 2
For our second argument, _____
_____.

Rebuttal 2
You incorrectly claim that _____
_____.

Disagree Argument 2
Instead, consider that _____
_____.

Rebuttal 2
To rebut your claim, allow us to mention that
_____.

Agree Argument 3
Our final argument in favor of this motion is
_____.

Rebuttal 3
The opposing team incorrectly believes
_____.

Disagree Argument 3
To give our final argument, _____
_____.

Agree Closing Statement
While the opposing team gave fine arguments, we ultimately believe that
_____
_____.

Disagree Closing Statement
In summation, _____
_____
_____.

Sum Up the Debate

Finish the debate summary.

AGREEING SIDE'S ARGUMENT

Our debate topic was _____.

The agree team's opinion was _____.

For their opening argument, they said _____.

To support this, they explained that _____
_____.

Second, they claimed _____.

For example, _____
_____.

Their closing argument was _____.

They mentioned _____
_____ to support their argument.

DISAGREEING SIDE'S ARGUMENT

In contrast, the con team claimed _____
_____.

For their opening argument, they stated that _____.

This argument was supported by _____
_____.

Second, they posited that _____.

They specifically mentioned _____
_____.

Their final argument was _____.

In detail, they explained that _____
_____.

Unit 06 Violent Video Games

A. Discuss the following questions as a class.
1. What do you see in the picture above?
2. What do you think the number 80 in the picture means?
3. Should violent video games have age restrictions?

B. Answer the following questions with a partner.
1. Do you like to play video games? If so, what types? If not, why not?
2. What are some positive aspects of playing video games?
3. Do you think violent video games always encourage violent behavior?

Unit 06   A   Learning about the Topic

Should violent video games be allowed for sale?

Read the passage and underline the main ideas.   Track 16

The first video games date back to the 1940s. However, it was not until 1993 with the release of the fighting game *Mortal Kombat* that video game violence became a major issue. Today, many lawmakers and parents blame video games for causing violent behavior in children and teenagers. Because of this, these groups would like to see violent video games banned. While not everyone is in favor of banning violent video games, there are many arguments suggesting that it is necessary.

One common reason given for banning violent video games is that they encourage aggressive behavior. Critics point out that video games are an **interactive** form of media. As video game players control their characters, they feel like they have a direct connection with their characters. As a result, players are more likely to **identify with** their characters. Because of this, they are more willing to copy the actions in the game. Second, children play violent video games more often than they see violent television shows or movies. The reason is that games are frequently marketed toward children. Children are not fully **mature**. So they may have a hard time distinguishing between reality and the fantasy world of games.

On the contrary, many people are not convinced that games are responsible for violent behavior. For one, there is little evidence that video games encourage violent behavior. In fact, some contend that violent video games may actually help children control feelings of anger and stress. One study was **conducted** by Harvard University. It found that nearly half of boys between the ages of 12 and 14 play violent video games to release their anger. Another benefit of video games is that they teach **practical** life skills. For example, first-person shooting games require players to work as teams. This requires good communication, strategy making, and cooperation skills.

Vocabulary Check

Choose the correct word for each definition.

| interactive | identify with | mature | conducted | practical |

1 to feel the same way as another person or thing _____
2 useful in everyday life _____
3 designed to respond to the actions of a user _____
4 being fully grown or developed _____
5 performed or done _____

Comprehension Questions

Check the correct answer for each question.

1 Why do some people want to ban violent video games?
   ☐ Because they encourage violent behavior
   ☐ Because they do not teach practical life skills

2 What makes video game players more likely to copy video game violence?
   ☐ The fact that many video games are marketed toward children
   ☐ The fact that players have direct connections with the game characters

3 What was the result of the Harvard study?
   ☐ That children who play games are more likely to be violent
   ☐ That children play games to release their anger and stress

4 What are some useful skills that video games teach?
   ☐ communication and cooperation skills
   ☐ goal making and staying calm under pressure

Questions for Debate

Think of and share ideas to explore the debatable issues in the article. Be sure to state your opinion clearly and to provide one supporting idea for each opinion.

1. Video games reward players for violent behavior. How can this lead to real world violence?

   From my perspective, it seems that _____
   _____.

   This is my opinion because _____
   _____.

2. Is the violence in video games more influential than the violence in movies and television shows?

   Speaking for myself, _____
   _____.

   The reason is _____
   _____.

3. Do you think video games are a good way to learn about skills such as strategy making?

   As far as I'm concerned, _____
   _____.

   To go into detail, _____
   _____.

4. Other than a violent video game ban, what are some other ways to control video game content?

   I think that _____
   _____.

   What I mean is _____
   _____.

5. As video game technology develops, do you think video game violence will become a larger issue?

   My opinion is _____
   _____.

   I feel this way because _____
   _____.

Opinion Examples

Look at the opinion examples about the motion below and answer the questions.

Motion: Violent video games should be banned.

Opinion A Track 17

A lot of parents and lawmakers complain that violent video games make children violent. From my perspective, playing violent video games is perfectly all right. Maybe a small number of children become more violent because of violent games. For most children, this is not the case. To share my experience, I played violent video games when I was younger. Even though I played first-person shooting games, I never tried to shoot anybody. Instead, playing games was a way for me to release my stress. Playing games with my friends also gave me memories that I'll appreciate forever.

Opinion B Track 18

As far as I'm concerned, violent video games need to be banned. These games reward players for committing crimes and even murder. Rewarding violent behavior is not a good message to send to anyone—not to children and not even to adults. It's not surprising to hear that murderers say that video games encouraged them to kill people. And violent video games may teach players communication and strategy skills. But they can also learn these skills by playing sports, which is healthier and more positive than playing video games. Banning violent video games will encourage more children to put down their controllers and to get active.

1. Underline the main idea of each opinion.

2. Which opinion is for the topic? Which one is against it?
   - FOR: _____
   - AGAINST: _____

3. What supporting ideas does each opinion give?
   - Opinion A: _____
   - Opinion B: _____

4. Create one more supporting idea for each argument.
   - Opinion A: _____
   - Opinion B: _____

Skills for Debate

Read and learn how to brainstorm your arguments.

How Can You Brainstorm Your Arguments?

To make logical arguments, you must **brainstorm logically**. When you brainstorm, you can write ideas for both your team and the opposing team. This can help you formulate **stronger arguments** for your debate. Once you create your arguments, you must **organize** your **ideas logically**. You should follow this pattern:

1. Think of ideas related to the topic (supporting arguments).
2. Decide whether the ideas are FOR or AGAINST the topic.
3. Write ideas that explain your arguments (reasons).
4. Think of ideas that explain your reasons (examples).

Practicing Debate Skills

Read the sample topics below. Then, brainstorm your ideas by following the steps above. An example is given to help you.

1 All children should be required to do household chores.

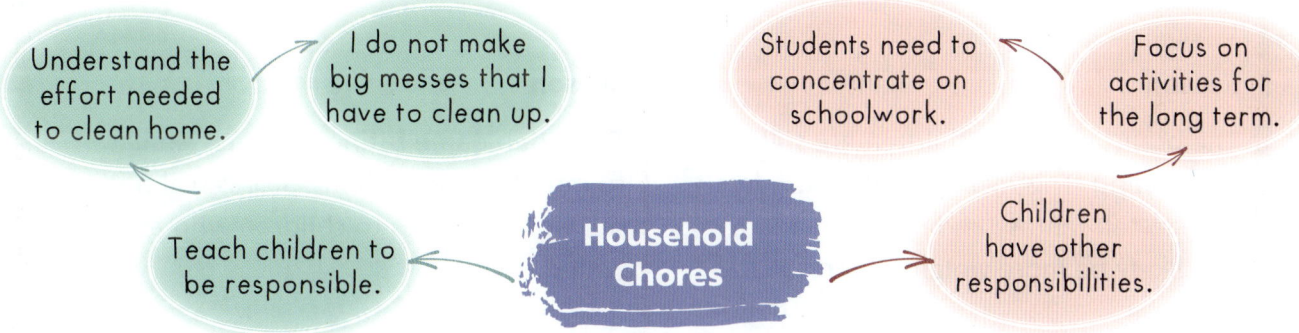

2 Violent video games should be banned.

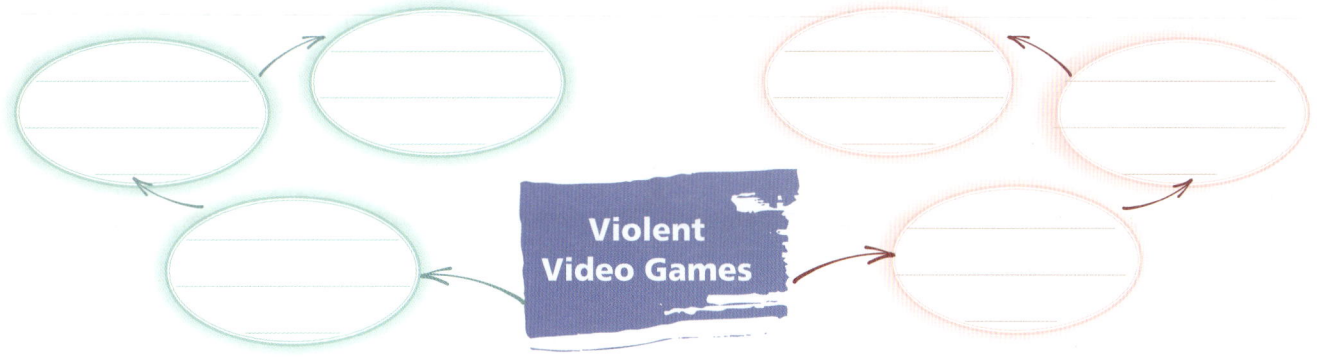

Unit 06 B Debating the Topic

Creating Your Debate

> **Motion: Violent video games should be banned.**

What are your arguments? Get into two groups and plan for the debate. Decide whether your team is FOR (agree) or AGAINST (disagree) the motion. Then, create your ARE: Argument, Reason, and Example. Use the example arguments below and the research from your workbook to help create your arguments.

■ Example Arguments

FOR

Argument

Children are likely to be exposed to violent video games at a young age, which can make them become violent.

Reason

The brains of young children are still developing. This means children are less able to tell fantasy and reality apart. They will likely be more violent as a result.

Example

According to the work of developmental biologist Jean Piaget, children are not capable of reasoning like adults until they are 15 years old.

AGAINST

Argument

Many countries have a ratings system that makes it illegal to sell violent video games to children.

Reason

The video game rating system is similar to movie rating systems. Stores will not sell violent games to children who are too young.

Example

A study done by the Entertainment Software Ratings Board (ESRB) in the United States found that 87 percent of video game stores would not sell mature-rated games to customers under the age of 17.

■ Arguments FOR/AGAINST the Motion

ARGUMENT 1

Argument
_____
_____
_____
_____
_____
_____

Reason
_____
_____
_____
_____
_____
_____

Example
_____
_____
_____
_____
_____
_____

ARGUMENT 2

Argument
_____
_____
_____
_____
_____
_____

Reason
_____
_____
_____
_____
_____
_____

Example
_____
_____
_____
_____
_____
_____

ARGUMENT 3

Argument
_____
_____
_____
_____
_____
_____

Reason
_____
_____
_____
_____
_____
_____

Example
_____
_____
_____
_____
_____
_____

Actual Debate

Now, it's time to debate. Use the flow chart below to help you organize the debate. The introductory expressions have been provided to help you. Put your arguments in logical order and make clear rebuttals to the opposing team's arguments.

Agree Opening Statement
It is our belief that _____ is beneficial.

Disagree Opening Statement
The advantages of _____ outweigh the drawbacks.

Agree Argument 1
For starters, consider that _____.

Rebuttal 1
It is the opposing team's belief that _____.
However, _____.

Disagree Argument 1
The primary shortcoming of _____ is _____.

Rebuttal 1
Your team claims that _____,
yet _____.

Agree Argument 2
We also support this motion because _____.

Rebuttal 2
It is wrong to assume that _____
because _____.

Disagree Argument 2
Next, let us point out that _____.

Rebuttal 2
Our team disagrees that _____.

Agree Argument 3
Our final argument is _____.

Rebuttal 3
In spite of your argument that _____,
we believe _____.

Disagree Argument 3
The final point we would like to make against this topic is _____.

Agree Closing Statement
Overall, we agree that _____.

Disagree Closing Statement
To sum up, it is the con team's belief that _____.

Sum Up the Debate

Finish the debate summary.

AGREEING SIDE'S ARGUMENT

Our debate today focused on _____.

The pro side's main argument was _____.

For their opening argument, they stated _____.

They supported this by explaining that _____
_____.

For their second argument, they presented _____.

To be specific, _____
_____.

The team concluded by arguing _____.

For example, _____
_____.

DISAGREEING SIDE'S ARGUMENT

In contrast, the second team argued _____
_____.

They started by claiming that _____.

This argument was supported by _____
_____.

Their next argument was _____.

They went into detail by explaining that _____
_____.

Their final point was _____.

Specifically, they mentioned _____
_____.

Chapter 4

Introducing an Argument Clearly

Unit 07 Giving Children Allowances

Unit 08 Elementary School Uniforms

Unit 07 Giving Children Allowances

WARM-UP

A. Discuss the following questions as a class.
1. What do you see in the picture above?
2. Why do you think the child is doing housework?
3. Should the boy be paid for the work he is doing? Why or why not?

B. Answer the following questions with a partner.
1. Do your parents make you do housework such as cleaning the dishes? If so, do they pay you for it?
2. What are some ways children can use the allowance money their parents give them?
3. Do you think it is better to give children a regular allowance or to have them work for their money?

Unit 07 A Learning about the Topic

Should parents give their children allowances?

Read the passage and underline the main ideas.  Track 19

By the time most children are six years old, they understand the concept of money. It is also around this age that many parents decide to give allowances to their children. Oftentimes, these allowances are **tied to** doing chores around the house such as taking out the trash and washing the dishes. Giving allowances for doing chores presents several benefits as well as disadvantages. Read on to find out what they are.

When children are given money for doing housework, they learn about the relationship between work and pay. As adults, people are rewarded for their work in the form of cash. Children learn this concept when they receive money for **chores**. But giving allowances for doing chores does not **solely** benefit children. Parents also **profit** because giving allowances encourages their children to do their chores better and more often. Another benefit of giving allowances is that children learn about the value of money. They can understand the amount of time and effort it takes to purchase items and that they need to save to buy larger items.

There are drawbacks to giving allowances to children. For one, giving allowances reduces children's feelings of responsibility toward their families. In one study, teenagers who were given allowances saw their chores simply as a way to make money. Instead, it is more important for children to learn that everyone in a family must **contribute** to its well-being and that doing chores is a part of this. Likewise, children may feel unmotivated to do even simple tasks around the house without being paid for them. An example is taking one's plate off the table after eating. This can lead children to argue unnecessarily with their parents over money. The worst situation is when parents give regular allowances not tied to chores. In this case, children expect money without having to earn it, which can make them greedy.

Vocabulary Check

Choose the correct word for each definition.

| be tied to | chore | solely | profit | contribute |

1 to get a benefit from something _____
2 to help cause something to happen _____
3 to be connected to something _____
4 a small job that is done regularly _____
5 only or just _____

Comprehension Questions

Check the correct answer for each question.

1 Why do some parents start giving allowances when their children are six years old?
   - ☐ Because their children usually start going to school
   - ☐ Because their children can understand the concept of money

2 What do children learn when they are given money for chores?
   - ☐ They learn the importance of helping out around the house.
   - ☐ They learn the relationship between working and earning money.

3 How do parents benefit from giving allowances to their children for doing chores?
   - ☐ Parents do not have to worry about buying items for their children.
   - ☐ Children will be more willing to do their chores regularly.

4 What is a possible drawback of giving money for doing chores?
   - ☐ Children may not be willing to do simple chores without being paid.
   - ☐ Children may expect more money for doing harder chores.

Questions for Debate

Think of and share ideas to explore the debatable issues in the article. Be sure to state your opinion clearly and to provide one supporting idea for each opinion.

1. Do you think six-year-olds should get allowances? If so, why? If not, what age is appropriate?

   I believe that _____
   _____.

   I hold this belief because _____
   _____.

2. How does giving allowances change the relationship between children and their parents?

   I feel that _____
   _____.

   This is due to the fact that _____
   _____.

3. What life lessons do children learn when they receive allowances?

   It seems to me that _____
   _____.

   For instance, _____
   _____.

4. Should parents decide how their children spend their allowances? Explain.

   I'm certain that _____
   _____.

   To explain more clearly, _____
   _____.

5. Should parents force their children to save part of their allowances? Why or why not?

   My impression is that _____
   _____.

   Let me clarify this by saying that _____
   _____.

Opinion Examples

Look at the opinion examples about the motion below and answer the questions.

Motion: Parents should give their children allowances.

Opinion A Track 20

Our society today is based on money. This means that everybody, especially children, needs to understand about money. Therefore, parents should definitely give their children allowances. Giving allowances makes children more independent. They don't need to ask their parents to buy every little toy and snack that they want. By spending their allowances, children learn to budget their money. They learn how to put aside money for larger purchases. But giving allowances only works if the parents are strict. They can't give more money if their children spend their allowances too quickly. And parents have to tie the allowances to chores.

Opinion B Track 21

Although giving allowances seems like a good idea, it simply does not work well in reality. When my parents gave me my allowance, I began expecting money for every little job they asked me to do. For example, my mom once asked me to take my plate to the sink after dinner. I asked her how much she would pay me to do that. My mom got really upset and told me that I should contribute to the household chores. By giving me an allowance, my mom taught me that I should be paid for everything I do. In my case, getting an allowance only made me greedy.

1 Underline the main idea of each opinion.

2 Which opinion is for the topic? Which one is against it?
- FOR: _____
- AGAINST: _____

3 What supporting ideas does each opinion give?
- Opinion A: _____
- Opinion B: _____

4 Create one more supporting idea for each argument.
- Opinion A: _____
- Opinion B: _____

Skills for Debate

Read and learn how to introduce your arguments clearly.

How Can You Introduce Your Arguments?

When you debate, it is important to state your opinion clearly. To do this, you should use introductory expressions. There are different expressions you use when you are FOR the topic and when you are AGAINST it. You should also use different expressions for your **opening statement**, **supporting arguments**, and **closing statement**. Here are some expressions that you should memorize and use in your debates.

Practicing Debate Skills

First, decide whether the expressions are for agreeing or disagreeing with a topic. Then, place the expressions in the correct order. Start with the opening statement, and then put the statements for the first, second, and third supporting arguments. Put the closing statement for each side last.

1. In conclusion, we disagree that
2. Furthermore, consider the drawbacks of
3. Our first argument in favor of the topic is
4. Finally, we feel . . . is true because
5. The final point we would like to make against this topic is
6. We, the members of the pro team, feel that
7. It is our opinion that . . . should be banned
8. Overall, we agree that
9. We also support this motion because
10. One problem caused by . . . is

Expressions FOR a topic

- _____
- _____
- _____
- _____
- _____

Expressions AGAINST a topic

- _____
- _____
- _____
- _____
- _____

Unit 07 B Debating the Topic

Creating Your Debate

> **Motion: Parents should give their children allowances.**

What are your arguments? Get into two groups and plan for the debate. Decide whether your team is FOR (agree) or AGAINST (disagree) the motion. Then, create your ARE: Argument, Reason, and Example. Use the example arguments below and the research from your workbook to help create your arguments.

■ Example Arguments

FOR

Argument

Giving allowances makes children become more independent.

Reason

Children who do not get allowances need to ask their parents to buy everything. By giving allowances, parents are teaching their children how to make their own purchasing decisions.

Example

My parents give me an allowance of 10,000 won a week. I have to use that money to buy school supplies, snacks, and so forth.

AGAINST

Argument

Children are too young to know how to spend money wisely.

Reason

Most of the important items a child needs, such as meals and clothing, are given by parents. Children are left to buy unnecessary and wasteful items.

Example

Many unhealthy products such as candy are marketed toward children. Young children would just follow advertisements and buy these unhealthy foods with their allowances.

Arguments FOR/AGAINST the Motion

ARGUMENT 1

Argument

Reason

Example

ARGUMENT 2

Argument

Reason

Example

ARGUMENT 3

Argument

Reason

Example

Actual Debate

Now, it's time to debate. Use the flow chart below to help you organize the debate.
The introductory expressions have been provided to help you. Put your arguments in logical order and make clear rebuttals to the opposing team's arguments.

Agree Opening Statement
We, the members of the pro team, believe that _____
_____ is beneficial.

Disagree Opening Statement
It is our opinion that _____
_____
_____ is harmful and unnecessary.

Agree Argument 1
For starters, consider that _____
_____
_____
_____
_____ .

Rebuttal 1
You said that _____
_____ , but consider that
_____
_____ .

Disagree Argument 1
The primary shortcoming of _____ is
_____
_____ .

Rebuttal 1
Your team's claim that _____
_____ is incorrect because
_____ .

Agree Argument 2
Second, it is undeniable that _____
_____
_____ .

Rebuttal 2
It is wrong to assume that _____
because _____ .

Disagree Argument 2
The next idea we would like you to consider
is _____ .

Rebuttal 2
Our team disagrees that _____
_____ .

Agree Argument 3
Finally, we feel that _____
_____ because
_____ .

Rebuttal 3
The opposing team's argument is incorrect
because _____
_____ .

Disagree Argument 3
The final point we would like to make against
this topic is _____
_____ .

Agree Closing Statement
To conclude, it is our opinion that _____
_____ .

Disagree Closing Statement
In brief, we disagree that _____
_____ .

Sum Up the Debate

Finish the debate summary.

AGREEING SIDE'S ARGUMENT

The topic of today's debate was _____.

The first team contended _____.

Their first argument was _____.

The example they gave was _____
_____.

For their second argument, they presented _____.

For instance, _____
_____.

Finally, the reasoned _____.

To share their example, _____
_____.

DISAGREEING SIDE'S ARGUMENT

The con team presented a different opinion _____
_____.

Their opening argument was _____.

This argument was supported by _____
_____.

Next, they explained _____.

In detail, _____
_____.

For their last argument, they contended _____.

They gave the example of _____
_____.

Unit 08 Elementary School Uniforms

A. Discuss the following questions as a class.

1. What do you see in the picture above?
2. Do you think the uniforms help the students concentrate on their studies?
3. How do you think the students feel about having to wear uniforms?

B. Answer the following questions with a partner.

1. Does your school require students to wear uniforms?
2. How can school uniforms make students feel part of a group?
3. Do you think students behave differently when they wear uniforms?

Unit 08 A Learning about the Topic

Should elementary schools also require school uniforms?

Read the passage and underline the main ideas.

 Track 22

The first school uniforms were introduced in Korea in 1886. At that time, only students in Western-style schools wore uniforms. Today, all middle and high schools in South Korea require students to wear uniforms. However, only a small number of elementary schools make their students wear uniforms. With all the advantages of school uniforms, elementary school officials should **consider** requiring their students to wear uniforms.

School uniforms can improve schools in several important ways. Many parents and school administrators agree that uniforms create a better academic environment. With uniforms, students do not have to worry about wearing trendy clothing. Instead, students can focus entirely on their studies. This is supported by statistics. Requiring uniforms on campus reduces **tardiness**, skipped classes, and general misbehavior. Moreover, uniforms promote school **pride**. Uniforms are similar to athletic team uniforms. They increase school spirit and unity and make students take their studies more seriously. Evidence also suggests that school uniforms create safer campuses. Students will not fight over their expensive jackets or accessories. At the same time, students from poorer backgrounds are less likely to be bullied.

There are just as many arguments against requiring school uniforms. Students complain that school uniforms **stifle** self-expression. Students want to be able to express themselves by wearing the clothes they like. This is especially true as students get older. However, school uniforms make this impossible. Parents also do not like the high cost of school uniforms. A single uniform often costs $250 or more. Parents generally buy two or more uniforms for their children each year. They also need to buy casual clothes in addition to uniforms, which adds to the cost. Finally, not all teachers believe that uniforms help reduce misbehavior. Several studies have suggested that requiring school uniforms does little to improve student behavior. The reason is that uniforms do not correct the **root** causes of misbehavior.

Vocabulary Check

Choose the correct word for each definition.

| consider | tardiness | pride | stifle | root |

1 to stop someone from doing something _____
2 to think about seriously _____
3 a feeling of happiness you get from a person or thing _____
4 arriving or doing something late _____
5 main or basic _____

Comprehension Questions

Check the correct answer for each question.

1 Which Korean students were the first to wear school uniforms?
  ☐ Those who were in middle and high school
  ☐ Those who were in Western-style schools

2 How do uniforms create better learning environments?
  ☐ They make it easy for students to get dressed in the morning.
  ☐ They allow students to concentrate only on their schoolwork.

3 Why do uniforms help make schools safer?
  ☐ Because students will not fight over clothing
  ☐ Because more students will participate in athletics

4 What is the main drawback of uniforms for students?
  ☐ Uniforms do not allow students to express themselves.
  ☐ Uniforms are too expensive to buy regularly.

Questions for Debate

Think of and share ideas to explore the debatable issues in the article. Be sure to state your opinion clearly and to provide one supporting idea for each opinion.

1. Beyond stopping fights between students, what are some other ways uniforms make schools safer?

   I believe that _____

   _____.

   I hold this belief because _____

   _____.

2. How can students express themselves in ways other than their clothing?

   In my opinion, _____

   _____.

   The reason I feel this way is _____

   _____.

3. What are some causes of student misbehavior that are not related to clothing?

   My belief is _____

   _____.

   To be more specific, _____

   _____.

4. Do you think elementary school students are more or less willing to wear school uniforms? Explain.

   It is my belief that _____

   _____.

   Let me explain this by mentioning _____

   _____.

5. Are school uniforms actually cheaper for parents in the long run? Why or why not?

   My impression is that _____

   _____.

   For example, _____

   _____.

Opinion Examples

Look at the opinion examples about the motion below and answer the questions.

> **Motion: Elementary schools should require school uniforms.**

Opinion A Track 23

Requiring school uniforms may be a good idea for older students, but they are not needed for elementary school students. Many of the problems middle and high schools face, such as fighting over clothing, do not occur in elementary schools. What's more, there is not much evidence that proves uniforms improve behavior in the first place. The same goes for grades. Test scores at schools with uniform policies are not much higher than at schools without them. The truth is that requiring students to wear uniforms will not make better learning environments. Students can study just as well in their regular clothing as they can in their uniforms.

Opinion B Track 24

More and more schools around the world are requiring their students to wear uniforms, and they are doing this for good reason. School uniforms are necessary to create proper educational environments. When students wear uniforms, they don't need to waste time choosing clothing in the morning. This means students have more time and energy to concentrate on their studies. We should also keep in mind that many adults wear uniforms to work. This can be a shirt with the company's name on it or a suit and tie. Wearing work uniforms helps people get their minds ready to work. For the same reason, all students should be required to wear uniforms.

1 Underline the main idea of each opinion.

2 Which opinion is for the topic? Which one is against it?
- FOR: _____
- AGAINST: _____

3 What supporting ideas does each opinion give?
- Opinion A: _____
- Opinion B: _____

4 Create one more supporting idea for each argument.
- Opinion A: _____
- Opinion B: _____

Skills for Debate

Read and learn how to introduce your arguments clearly.

How Can You Introduce Your Arguments?

When you introduce your points, it is important to use **clear expressions**. A strong introductory expression generally has **three main components**. The first is the **transition**. A transition lets the listener know which argument you are introducing by using words such as "first," "next," and "lastly." Next, your introductory phrase should have a **clear subject**. Some good subjects are "we," "our team," and "the members." The final component is the **opinion phrase**. The opinion phrase should obviously state your team's opinion about the topic. Some phrases you can use are "agree/disagree," "for/against," and "support/refute." Use many different expressions to give your speech variety.

Practicing Debate Skills

Read each of the introductory expressions below. Then, rewrite each expression in two different ways. Be sure that the meaning stays the same. Some words have been given to help you.

1. It is the opinion of the pro team that . . .

    A As the members of the pro team, _____

    B _____

2. Our first argument is . . .

    A Our opening _____

    B _____

3. The next point we would like to mention is . . .

    A _____, please consider that _____

    B _____

4. Finally, it is evident that . . .

    A For our final argument, _____

    B _____

5. Overall, we believe that . . .

    A To summarize, _____

    B _____

Unit 08 B Debating the Topic

Creating Your Debate

Motion: Elementary schools should require school uniforms.

What are your arguments? Get into two groups and plan for the debate. Decide whether your team is FOR (agree) or AGAINST (disagree) the motion. Then, create your ARE: Argument, Reason, and Example. Use the example arguments below and the research from your workbook to help create your arguments.

■ Example Arguments

FOR

Argument

Uniforms allow students to do better on their studies.

Reason

By requiring school uniforms, students do not have to worry about their clothing. Instead, they can focus all their energy on their schoolwork. This improves their test scores.

Example

A study done by Ohio State University found that schools with uniforms had an increase in their students' test scores over a three-year period. During the same time, schools without uniforms saw a decrease in their students' test scores.

AGAINST

Argument

Problems of bullying over clothing generally do not occur in elementary schools.

Reason

Elementary school children are too young to worry about fashion. The clothing that elementary school students wear has little influence over their behavior.

Example

Many middle and high schools adopted uniforms in response to fights between bullies and other students. However, elementary school students are less likely to get into fights.

■ Arguments FOR/AGAINST the Motion

ARGUMENT 1	ARGUMENT 2	ARGUMENT 3
Argument	**Argument**	**Argument**
Reason	**Reason**	**Reason**
Example	**Example**	**Example**

Actual Debate

Now, it's time to debate. Use the flow chart below to help you organize the debate.
The introductory expressions have been provided to help you. Put your arguments in logical order and make clear rebuttals to the opposing team's arguments.

Agree Opening Statement
Our belief is that _____.

Agree Argument 1
For starters, consider that _____.

Rebuttal 1
You said that _____, but we believe that _____.

Agree Argument 2
We also support this motion because _____.

Rebuttal 2
You said that _____, but we think _____.

Agree Argument 3
For our last argument, let us point out that _____.

Agree Closing Statement
To conclude, the pro team believes that _____.

Disagree Opening Statement
We disagree with the motion that _____.

Rebuttal 1
You said that _____.
However, _____.

Disagree Argument 1
Our first reason is _____.

Rebuttal 2
It is wrong to assume that _____ since _____.

Disagree Argument 2
It is also necessary to consider that _____.

Rebuttal 3
While the opposing team claims that _____, we believe that _____.

Disagree Argument 3
The final point we would like to make against this topic is _____.

Disagree Closing Statement
In conclusion, we disagree that _____.

Sum Up the Debate

Finish the debate summary.

AGREEING SIDE'S ARGUMENT

Today's debate motion was _____.

The pro team argued _____.

Their first argument was _____.

They supported this by explaining that _____
_____.

Next, the team posited _____.

Their claim was supported by _____
_____.

Their closing argument was _____.

They mentioned _____
_____ to strengthen their argument.

DISAGREEING SIDE'S ARGUMENT

The second team argued differently. They felt _____
_____.

For their opening argument _____.

This argument was supported by _____
_____.

Second, the con team stated _____.

For example, _____
_____.

Their final point was _____.

This was explained by _____
_____.

Chapter 5

Listing Supporting Arguments

Unit 09 English as the World Language

Unit 10 Social Networking Sites for Education

Unit 09 English as the World Language

A. Discuss the following questions as a class.

1. What do you see in the picture above?
2. Which of the languages can you name?
3. What problems are created by having many different languages in the world?

B. Answer the following questions with a partner.

1. Do you enjoy learning foreign languages? Why or why not?
2. How can having a single world language improve relationships between nations?
3. What are some possible problems of having a single world language?

Unit 09 A Learning about the Topic

Should everybody in the world speak English?

Read the passage and underline the main ideas. Track 25

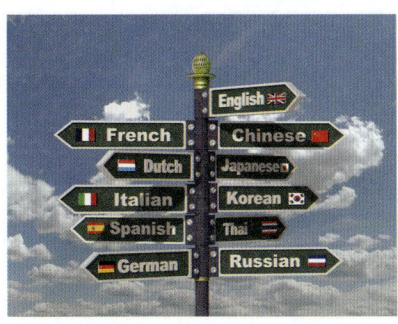

Throughout history, several languages have been considered world languages. In ancient Europe, Greek was widely used. From the first to the seventeenth centuries, Latin was commonly spoken. From then until the twentieth century, the international language was French. Today, the most **widespread** language is English, with over one billion speakers. Would the world be a better place if everybody spoke English? Not necessarily.

One disadvantage of having everybody speak English would be a lack of **diversity**. If everyone spoke English as their main language, the world's cultures would become more similar. This would make the world a less interesting place. Likewise, having a world language would mean a loss of cultural identity. Language is closely linked to a nation's culture and history. Oftentimes, these cultural ideas do not translate into other languages. A good example would be the Korean word *jeong*, which does not directly translate into English. Finally, if everyone in the world tries to learn English, different forms of English will appear that not all English speakers can understand. This already happens today with **dialects** such as Singlish, the English of Singapore. Only people from Singapore can properly understand Singlish.

Many people believe that English has already become the world language. For starters, hundreds of companies and organizations use English as their working language. Companies such as Samsung and organizations such as the United Nations use English to do their business. The obvious benefit of using English for international business is that there will be fewer chances for miscommunication. When translation and **interpretation** are used, there is an increased chance of people misunderstanding each other. This is not an issue if everyone speaks English. Furthermore, learning English does not have to mean giving up one's national language. For example, millions of Indians are able to speak English at a conversational level. At the same time, India has dozens of **domestic** languages which are spoken in daily life.

Vocabulary Check

Choose the correct word for each definition.

| widespread | diversity | dialect | interpretation | domestic |

1. the state of having many different types _____
2. the act of translating one language into another _____
3. a form of a language specific to an area _____
4. of or within your own country _____
5. common in many different places _____

Comprehension Questions

Check the correct answer for each question.

1. Which language was a world language for the longest period of time?
   - ☐ Greek
   - ☐ Latin
   - ☐ French
   - ☐ English

2. How could a world language affect the cultures of the world?
   - ☐ It could lead to a loss of cultural identity.
   - ☐ It could allow all cultures to become widespread.

3. What is true of the English of Singapore?
   - ☐ It includes vocabulary words that cannot be translated into English.
   - ☐ It cannot be understood by people who are not from Singapore.

4. Why do some companies use English as their working language?
   - ☐ Because it is the language spoken by the most people
   - ☐ Because it decreases the chances of misunderstandings occurring

Questions for Debate

Think of and share ideas to explore the debatable issues in the article. Be sure to state your opinion clearly and to provide one supporting idea for each opinion.

1 What are some problems that could occur if every nation forced its people to speak English?

From my perspective, it seems that _____
_____.

The reason I feel this way is _____
_____.

2 Would having a world language make the world a more peaceful place? Why or why not?

I feel that _____
_____.

To illustrate this, let me mention _____
_____.

3 What are some ways in which a world language would affect the cultures of different nations?

It seems to me that _____
_____.

To go into detail, _____
_____.

4 Do you think English could become the language of the West and Chinese the language of the East?

It is my opinion that _____
_____.

I have this opinion because _____
_____.

5 Should nations try to keep their domestic languages like India, or should they only use English? Explain.

To me, it is clear that _____
_____.

For example, _____
_____.

Opinion Examples

Look at the opinion examples about the motion below and answer the questions.

Motion: English should become the world language.

Opinion A Track 26

It is my opinion that everyone in the world should speak English. If everyone spoke English, there would be much less miscommunication in the world. People could understand each other better. Part of the reason is there would be fewer translation errors. Another reason is that people's ways of thinking and logic are based on their language. By having everyone speak English, our ways of thinking would become more similar. Finally, making English the world language doesn't mean that people have to stop speaking other languages. They could simply speak English in addition to their other languages.

Opinion B Track 27

There have been many attempts to create a world language in the past. But do you know what? None of these attempts has ever been successful. If English becomes the world language, there will always be some people who don't speak it. Some people just won't have access to educational opportunities to learn the language. The result of this will actually be a less unified society, with English speakers separated from non-English speakers. You also have to consider the costs. Making more English classes, putting English on all the signs, and doing other similar activities would cost a lot of time and money.

1 Underline the main idea of each opinion.

2 Which opinion is for the topic? Which one is against it?
- FOR: _____
- AGAINST: _____

3 What supporting ideas does each opinion give?
- Opinion A: _____
- Opinion B: _____

4 Create one more supporting idea for each argument.
- Opinion A: _____
- Opinion B: _____

Skills for Debate

Read and learn how to create supporting arguments that are strong.

How Can You Create Strong Supporting Arguments?

Arguments are the heart of a debate. They are the ideas that prove why your motion is correct. However, students often have a hard time making arguments that they can **support**. They often state ideas that are **opinions, facts,** or are **not directly related to the topic**. To avoid this, you should make sure that each of your arguments is **debatable** and **supportable**. There must be arguments both in favor of and against your arguments. You must also be able to support them with **reasons** and **examples**.

Practicing Debate Skills

The arguments below are not good arguments. Rewrite them to make them debatable. Then, think of a brief supporting reason or example for each argument. An example has been given to help you.

1 I like action movies the most.
- Rewrite: <u>Action movies are the most exciting type of film.</u>
- Support: <u>Action movies are fast paced. They contain explosions, fights, and other interesting events.</u>

2 Statistics show that 35 percent of children in the U.S. are raised by single parents.
- Rewrite: _____
- Support: _____

3 Dogs and cats are the most popular pets in people's homes.
- Rewrite: _____
- Support: _____

4 Fruits and vegetables are lower in fat and calories than meats.
- Rewrite: _____
- Support: _____

Unit 09 B Debating the Topic

Creating Your Debate

Motion: English should become the world language.

What are your arguments? Get into two groups and plan for the debate. Decide whether your team is FOR (agree) or AGAINST (disagree) the motion. Then, create your ARE: Argument, Reason, and Example. Use the example arguments below and the research from your workbook to help create your arguments.

■ Example Arguments

FOR

Argument

There will be fewer communication problems if everybody speaks English.

Reason

When people cannot speak the same language, they can hardly communicate. When everybody speaks English, it will be easier to do something as simple as ordering a meal or as complex as negotiating a contract.

Example

Most of the European Union uses English to make doing politics and business easier.

AGAINST

Argument

Keeping different languages reflects the diversity of the world's cultures.

Reason

A nation's culture and language tie into each other. You cannot have one without the other.

Example

Some politicians have tried to make English the national language in Korea. Their efforts have failed because the Korean mindset, culture, and history are based on the Korean language.

■ Arguments FOR/AGAINST the Motion

ARGUMENT 1

Argument

Reason

Example

ARGUMENT 2

Argument

Reason

Example

ARGUMENT 3

Argument

Reason

Example

Actual Debate

Now, it's time to debate. Use the flow chart below to help you organize the debate.
The introductory expressions have been provided to help you. Put your arguments in logical order and make clear rebuttals to the opposing team's arguments.

Agree Opening Statement
It is our team's opinion that _____
_____.

Disagree Opening Statement
Unlike the pro team, we feel that _____
_____.

Agree Argument 1
Our first argument is _____
_____
_____
_____.

Rebuttal 1
Your team claims that _____.
However, _____.

Disagree Argument 1
To give our first argument, _____
_____.

Rebuttal 1
While the con team claims _____
_____,
we feel that _____
_____.

Rebuttal 2
You incorrectly believe that _____
_____
_____.

Agree Argument 2
Next, we believe that _____
_____.

Disagree Argument 2
To add to our first argument, _____
_____
_____.

Rebuttal 2
You stated that _____
_____.
Nevertheless, _____
_____.

Rebuttal 3
Our opponents claim _____
_____.
The truth of the matter is _____
_____.

Agree Argument 3
For our last argument, let us point out that
_____.

Disagree Argument 3
Our final point is _____
_____.

Agree Closing Statement
Overall, our team holds that _____
_____.

Disagree Closing Statement
In conclusion, we are against the idea that
_____.

Sum Up the Debate

Finish the debate summary.

AGREEING SIDE'S ARGUMENT

The debate motion for today was _____.

The pro team started off by arguing that _____.

For their opening argument, they mentioned _____.

The reasoning was _____
_____.

The agreeing team's second idea was _____.

Their claim was supported by _____
_____.

Finally, they reasoned that _____.

For instance, _____
_____.

DISAGREEING SIDE'S ARGUMENT

The second side, on the other hand, argued that _____
_____.

Their first argument was that _____.

For example, _____
_____.

Their second reason was that _____.

For instance, _____
_____.

Finally, they explained that _____.

They illustrated this by mentioning that _____
_____.

Unit 10
Social Networking Sites for Education

WARM-UP

A. Discuss the following questions as a class.
1. What do you see in the picture above?
2. Why does the image include a map of the world?
3. How does social networking allow people to keep in touch more easily?

B. Answer the following questions with a partner.
1. Do you use any social networking sites? If so, which ones do you use?
2. What are some other ways social networking sites can be used in addition to socializing?
3. How have the Internet and other technology changed the way students learn?

Unit 10 A Learning about the Topic

Should social networking sites be used in education?

Read the passage and underline the main ideas.

 Track 28

Each day, millions of students log onto Facebook and Twitter. They send messages to their friends close to home and around the world. These social networking sites allow people to connect and communicate more easily than ever before. Most people view social networking sites only as ways to make friends, to play games, and to have fun. However, they can also be wonderful tools to use in the classroom to encourage learning.

Connectivity is the greatest benefit offered by social networking sites. With social networking sites, students can easily contact each other. This way, they can discuss their schoolwork and academic interests. For example, students can make Facebook groups about their schoolwork. Social networking sites also allow parents to **keep track of** their children's education more easily. Parents can easily see what their children are learning in school. They can do this by visiting their children's **profiles**. They can also contact their children's teachers. A final benefit is that social networking sites promote group discussion. Sites such as Twitter encourage users to share whatever ideas are on their mind. Students may be more willing to share their true opinions than in a traditional classroom setting.

Some remain **skeptical** of using social networking sites for education. The most common counterargument is that social networks actually distract students from learning. For every page related to academics, there are dozens more about pop singers, movies, and video games. Critics also argue that social networking sites **hinder** real-world socialization. Most students never actually meet their so-called friends and know very little about them. This can lead to another problem of social networking: They can promote poor discussion skills. People often make **outrageous** or silly comments on social networking sites. Students might, for example, make extreme arguments since they are not facing their teacher and classmates. This type of discussion often prevents learning from happening.

Vocabulary Check

Choose the correct word for each definition.

| keep track of | profile | skeptical | hinder | outrageous |

1 to make a task slow and difficult _____

2 to know about and follow _____

3 a description containing information about a person _____

4 surprising or shocking _____

5 having doubt about the truth of something _____

Comprehension Questions

Check the correct answer for each question.

1 What do most people think about social networking sites?

☐ They are only used for making friends, playing games, and having fun.
☐ They are important tools for teachers to use in the classroom.

2 How could parents benefit from using social networking sites in education?

☐ They could make lesson plans for their children to follow.
☐ They could easily see what their children learn in school.

3 How can social networking sites hinder learning?

☐ They can distract students with information about pop singers and movies.
☐ They can make it harder for students to talk with people in person.

4 Why are students less likely to make outrageous comments in a classroom?

☐ Because they would have less time to think about their comments
☐ Because they would face their teacher and classmates

Questions for Debate

Think of and share ideas to explore the debatable issues in the article. Be sure to state your opinion clearly and to provide one supporting idea for each opinion.

1 What are some ways students can use social networking sites to help them learn?

It is my opinion that _____
_____.

For instance, _____
_____.

2 How old should students be in order to use social networking sites for schoolwork?

From my view, it seems that _____
_____.

This can be illustrated by _____
_____.

3 Do you think that most students ever use social networks to help them study or learn?

In my opinion, _____
_____.

To be more specific, _____
_____.

4 How can social networking sites encourage learning on a global scale?

I believe that _____
_____.

The reason is that _____
_____.

5 How important is learning how to use technology in today's society?

My belief is that _____
_____.

Consider that _____
_____.

Opinion Examples

Look at the opinion examples about the motion below and answer the questions.

Motion: Social networking is beneficial for education.

Opinion A Track 29

Using technology in the classroom is a great idea. This does not mean that social networking sites should be included. Social networking sites were originally made to help people make friends. They can be used for learning, but that isn't their main purpose. So when students go on social networking sites, they forget about their studies and just waste time talking to friends. What's worse is that students can become addicted to these sites. They can spend hours a day surfing Facebook instead of actually studying. This goes against the idea of using social networking sites to study in the first place.

Opinion B Track 30

People who think social networking sites can't be helpful for learning do not know their full value. First of all, social networking sites are very customizable. You can join groups related to your specific interests. For example, if you like learning about history, you can join history groups. And let's not forget the connectivity of social networking sites. You can send messages to all your classmates in a matter of seconds with social networking sites. Plus, you can connect with your teachers and parents. Besides, social networking sites won't replace traditional classrooms. They'll just be another tool for teachers to use.

1 Underline the main idea of each opinion.

2 Which opinion is for the topic? Which one is against it?
- FOR: _____
- AGAINST: _____

3 What supporting ideas does each opinion give?
- Opinion A: _____
- Opinion B: _____

4 Create one more supporting idea for each argument.
- Opinion A: _____
- Opinion B: _____

Skills for Debate

Read and learn how to create supporting arguments that are strong.

How Can You Create Strong Supporting Arguments?

To debate effectively, you need to create supporting arguments. However, not all supporting arguments are convincing. **Weak supporting arguments do not clearly prove** your team's motion. They may be a **simple fact** that you cannot support with examples, **too broad**, or **not clearly related** to the topic. In contrast, **strong arguments clearly prove** your motion and can be supported by reasons and examples. When making your debate, try to use strong arguments as often as possible.

Practicing Debate Skills

Read the sample motion below. Then, read the arguments in favor of the motion. Decide if they are weak or strong and explain why. If the arguments are weak, rewrite them to make them stronger. If they are strong, write a brief supporting reason or example.

Sample Motion: Social networking is a great educational tool.

1. Social networking sites were first created to make friends online. (☐ STRONG ☐ WEAK)
   → _____

2. Using technology in the classroom makes students interested in learning. (☐ STRONG ☐ WEAK)
   → _____

3. Social networking sites can help teachers, parents, and students connect. (☐ STRONG ☐ WEAK)
   → _____

4. Facebook is one of the most popular websites in the world. (☐ STRONG ☐ WEAK)
   → _____

Unit 10 B Debating the Topic

Creating Your Debate

Motion: Social networking is beneficial for education.

What are your arguments? Get into two groups and plan for the debate. Decide whether your team is FOR (agree) or AGAINST (disagree) the motion. Then, create your ARE: Argument, Reason, and Example. Use the example arguments below and the research from your workbook to help create your arguments.

■ Example Arguments

FOR

Argument

Teachers can use social networking sites to make learning simpler.

Reason

Social networking sites allow teachers to assign students smaller tasks easily. These smaller tasks are easy to complete but still move students toward a larger learning goal.

Example

Instead of asking students to write full book reports, teachers can ask students to find videos online related to their books. Fun tasks such as these make students want to learn.

AGAINST

Argument

Students will be too distracted to learn if they use social networking sites.

Reason

Most of the content on social networking sites is not related to studying. Most posts are about celebrities or silly news stories. This does not help students learn.

Example

The most common status update terms on Facebook deal with celebrity news, sports, and people's personal lives. None of the most popular terms are academic in nature.

Arguments FOR/AGAINST the Motion

ARGUMENT 1

Argument

Reason

Example

ARGUMENT 2

Argument

Reason

Example

ARGUMENT 3

Argument

Reason

Example

Actual Debate

Now, it's time to debate. Use the flow chart below to help you organize the debate.
The introductory expressions have been provided to help you. Put your arguments in logical order and make clear rebuttals to the opposing team's arguments.

Agree Opening Statement
Today, we will explain why _____
_____.

Agree Argument 1
First of all, _____
_____
_____
_____.

Rebuttal 1
In spite of your claim that _____
_____,
we believe that _____
_____.

Agree Argument 2
For our second argument, consider that _____
_____
_____.

Rebuttal 2
You said that _____
_____.
Even so, _____
_____
_____.

Agree Argument 3
Finally, we must point out that _____
_____
_____.

Agree Closing Statement
Overall, our team contends that _____
_____
_____.

Disagree Opening Statement
We disagree with the pro team that _____
_____.

Rebuttal 1
You believe that _____.
This is incorrect because _____.

Disagree Argument 1
Our first argument is that _____
_____.

Rebuttal 2
Your team wrongly claims that _____
_____
_____.

Disagree Argument 2
In addition, we believe that _____
_____
_____.

Rebuttal 3
While our opponents feel that _____
_____,
we feel that _____
_____.

Disagree Argument 3
Lastly, it must be mentioned that _____
_____
_____.

Disagree Closing Statement
In conclusion, we disagree that _____
_____
_____.

Sum Up the Debate

Finish the debate summary.

AGREEING SIDE'S ARGUMENT

Today's debate dealt with _____.

The pro team began by arguing that _____.

Their first argument was _____.

They explained this by mentioning _____
_____.

For their second idea, the agree side argued that _____.

For example, _____
_____.

Finally, they reasoned that _____.

For instance, _____
_____.

DISAGREEING SIDE'S ARGUMENT

The con team felt differently. They claimed that _____
_____.

For their first argument, they said that _____.

Specifically, they mentioned that _____
_____.

Their second reason was that _____.

For example, _____
_____.

To finish their argument, the con side mentioned that _____.

The example they gave was _____
_____.

Instilling Knowledge and Skills
for Thoughtful Debate

DEBATE Pro

Book 1

Jonathan S. McClelland

Workbook

DEBATE Pro
Book 1

Workbook

Contents

How to Use This Book _4

Unit 01 Year-Round Schools _6

Unit 02 Keeping Pets _10

Unit 03 Banning Junk Food in Schools _14

Unit 04 Animal Testing _18

Unit 05 Beauty Pageants _22

Unit 06 Violent Video Games _26

Unit 07 Giving Children Allowances _30

Unit 08 Elementary School Uniforms _34

Unit 09 English as the World Language _38

Unit 10 Social Networking Sites for Education _42

How to Use This Book

Overview

The workbook is intended to supplement the main book both during class and for homework. It provides space for students to take notes during class and to do additional research outside of class.

Introduction for each section

Organizing Ideas

This part requires students to analyze the reading passage from the main book and write down each of the arguments and examples for and against the topic.

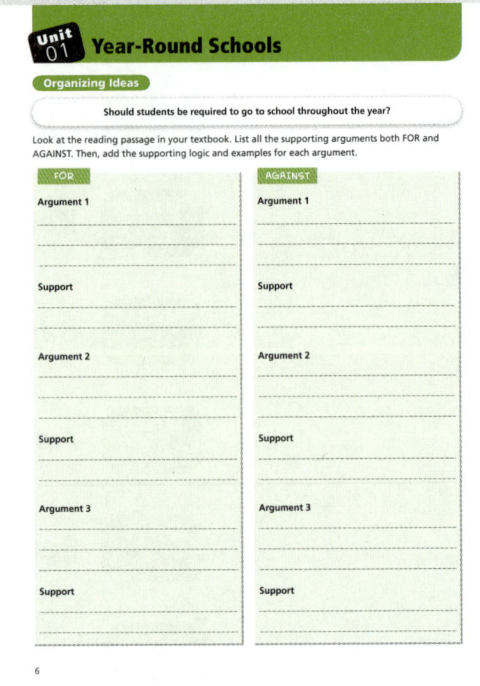

Making Supporting Examples

This section helps students develop their skills in making examples. In each book, five types of examples are explained: statistics, expert opinions, facts, academic studies, and personal opinions.

Additional Research

This section provides students with additional information about the topic based on the type of example explained in the previous section. The information is followed by four brief comprehension questions. Sample phrases are provided to help students create their answers.

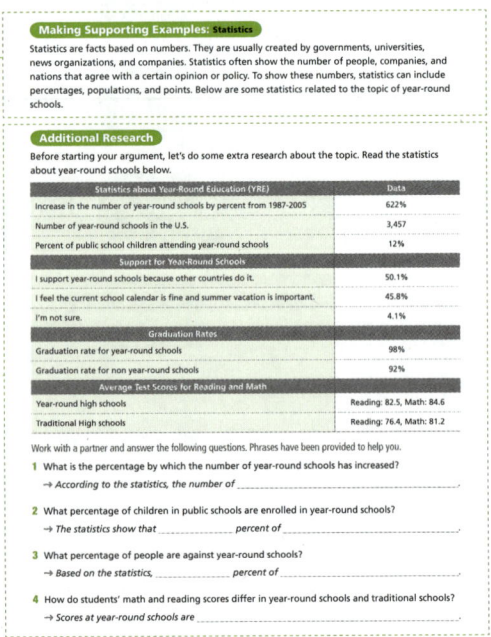

Your Research

In this section, students are asked to do additional research outside of class. They are encouraged to find information from magazines, newspapers, or academic websites and to write or tape the material in the space provided. Based on the information they find, students are asked to create four additional examples which they can use during their debate.

Debate Note-Taking

This section provides space which students can use to take notes during the debate.

Peer Evaluation

This part requires students to evaluate their peers' debate performance. Eight criteria are provided along with a ten-point scale for each criterion with a total maximum score of eighty points for each student.

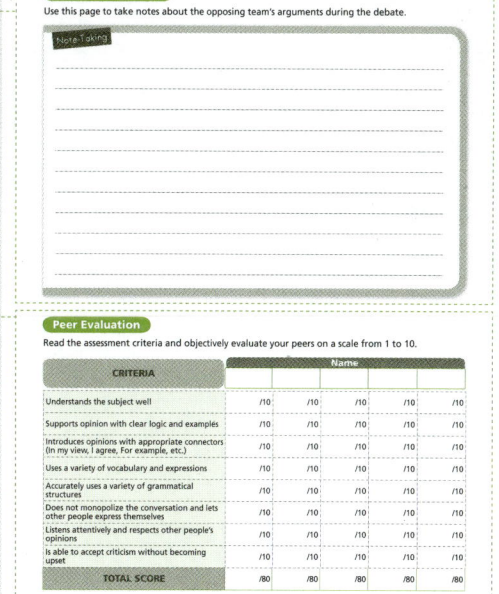

Unit 01 Year-Round Schools

Organizing Ideas

Should students be required to go to school throughout the year?

Look at the reading passage in your textbook. List all the supporting arguments both FOR and AGAINST. Then, add the supporting logic and examples for each argument.

FOR	AGAINST
Argument 1	**Argument 1**
Support	**Support**
Argument 2	**Argument 2**
Support	**Support**
Argument 3	**Argument 3**
Support	**Support**

Making Supporting Examples: Statistics

Statistics are facts based on numbers. They are usually created by governments, universities, news organizations, and companies. Statistics often show the number of people, companies, and nations that agree with a certain opinion or policy. To show these numbers, statistics can include percentages, populations, and points. Below are some statistics related to the topic of year-round schools.

Additional Research

Before starting your argument, let's do some extra research about the topic. Read the statistics about year-round schools below.

Statistics about Year-Round Education (YRE)	Data
Increase in the number of year-round schools by percent from 1987-2005	622%
Number of year-round schools in the U.S.	3,457
Percent of public school children attending year-round schools	12%
Support for Year-Round Schools	
I support year-round schools because other countries do it.	50.1%
I feel the current school calendar is fine and summer vacation is important.	45.8%
I'm not sure.	4.1%
Graduation Rates	
Graduation rate for year-round schools	98%
Graduation rate for non year-round schools	92%
Average Test Scores for Reading and Math	
Year-round high schools	Reading: 82.5, Math: 84.6
Traditional High schools	Reading: 76.4, Math: 81.2

Work with a partner and answer the following questions. Phrases have been provided to help you.

1. What is the percentage by which the number of year-round schools has increased?
   → According to the statistics, the number of _____.

2. What percentage of children in public schools are enrolled in year-round schools?
   → The statistics show that _____ percent of _____.

3. What percentage of people are against year-round schools?
   → Based on the statistics, _____ percent of _____.

4. How do students' math and reading scores differ in year-round schools and traditional schools?
   → Scores at year-round schools are _____.

Your Research

Find an article about year-round schools from a magazine, newspaper, or academic website. Paste or tape the article in your workbook in the space below.

Use your article and write four specific examples or pieces of evidence you can use for your debate. Try to include different types of examples, including opinion polls, statistics, academic studies, and general facts.

- _____
- _____
- _____
- _____

Debate Note-Taking

Use this page to take notes about the opposing team's arguments during the debate.

Note-Taking

_____
_____
_____
_____
_____
_____
_____
_____
_____
_____
_____

Peer Evaluation

Read the assessment criteria and objectively evaluate your peers on a scale from 1 to 10.

CRITERIA	Name				
Understands the subject well	/10	/10	/10	/10	/10
Supports opinion with clear logic and examples	/10	/10	/10	/10	/10
Introduces opinions with appropriate connectors (In my view, I agree, For example, etc.)	/10	/10	/10	/10	/10
Uses a variety of vocabulary and expressions	/10	/10	/10	/10	/10
Accurately uses a variety of grammatical structures	/10	/10	/10	/10	/10
Does not monopolize the conversation and lets other people express themselves	/10	/10	/10	/10	/10
Listens attentively and respects other people's opinions	/10	/10	/10	/10	/10
Is able to accept criticism without becoming upset	/10	/10	/10	/10	/10
TOTAL SCORE	/80	/80	/80	/80	/80

Unit 02 Keeping Pets

Organizing Ideas

Should people be allowed to keep animals as pets?

Look at the reading passage in your textbook. List all the supporting arguments both FOR and AGAINST. Then, add the supporting logic and examples for each argument.

FOR

Argument 1
_____
_____
_____

Support
_____
_____
_____

Argument 2
_____
_____
_____

Support
_____
_____
_____

Argument 3
_____
_____
_____

Support
_____
_____
_____

AGAINST

Argument 1
_____
_____
_____

Support
_____
_____
_____

Argument 2
_____
_____
_____

Support
_____
_____
_____

Argument 3
_____
_____
_____

Support
_____
_____
_____

Making Supporting Examples: Expert Opinions

Expert opinions are usually the ideas and opinions of experts in a given field. Experts are typically people such as professors, doctors, and business managers. Most experts base their opinions on their years of experience doing researching and working in their fields. Below are some expert opinions related to the topic of keeping pets.

Additional Research

Before starting your argument, let's do some extra research about the topic. Read the expert opinions about keeping pets.

> As a medical doctor, I often encourage my patients to get pets. Here are just some of the health benefits of having a pet.
>
> **Lower Blood Pressure**
> Research strongly suggests that keeping a pet can lower high blood pressure that is caused by stress. In one study, 30 business managers were given treatments for their high blood pressure. Each member of one group was given a dog or cat as a pet. Every member of the other group was given some high blood pressure medicine. The group whose members were given pets had much lower blood pressure after just one month compared to the members of the other group.
>
> **Reduced Risk of Allergies and Asthma**
> Being exposed to animals from a young age lowers a person's chance of having allergies or asthma. Scientists believe this happens because a person's immune system becomes stronger against allergens such as cat dander.
>
> **A Stronger Heart**
> A major study of heart attack survivors found that survivors with a pet had just a 1 percent chance of dying one year after their heart attack. In contrast, those without a pet had an 8 percent chance of dying. Another study found that people who have owned a cat decreased their chance of having a heart attack by more than 35 percent.

Work with a partner and answer the following questions. Phrases have been provided to help you.

1 What happened to the business managers who got a pet dog or cat?

→ *The research shows that* _____.

2 How does keeping pets reduce a person's chance of suffering allergies?

→ *This happens because* _____.

3 What does the doctor say about the study of heart attack survivors?

→ *The doctor says that heart attack survivors with a pet* _____

compared to non-pet owners who _____.

4 How does owning a cat improve one's health?

→ *One study found that* _____.

Your Research

Find an article about keeping pets from a magazine, newspaper, or academic website. Paste or tape the article in your workbook in the space below.

Paste or Tape Your Research Article Here

Use your article and write four specific examples or pieces of evidence you can use for your debate. Try to include different types of examples, including opinion polls, statistics, academic studies, and general facts.

- _____
- _____
- _____
- _____

Debate Note-Taking

Use this page to take notes about the opposing team's arguments during the debate.

Note-Taking

_____
_____
_____
_____
_____
_____
_____
_____
_____
_____
_____
_____
_____

Peer Evaluation

Read the assessment criteria and objectively evaluate your peers on a scale from 1 to 10.

CRITERIA	Name				
Understands the subject well	/10	/10	/10	/10	/10
Supports opinion with clear logic and examples	/10	/10	/10	/10	/10
Introduces opinions with appropriate connectors (In my view, I agree, For example, etc.)	/10	/10	/10	/10	/10
Uses a variety of vocabulary and expressions	/10	/10	/10	/10	/10
Accurately uses a variety of grammatical structures	/10	/10	/10	/10	/10
Does not monopolize the conversation and lets other people express themselves	/10	/10	/10	/10	/10
Listens attentively and respects other people's opinions	/10	/10	/10	/10	/10
Is able to accept criticism without becoming upset	/10	/10	/10	/10	/10
TOTAL SCORE	/80	/80	/80	/80	/80

Unit 03 — Banning Junk Food in Schools

Organizing Ideas

> Should schools get rid of junk food from their lunchrooms?

Look at the reading passage in your textbook. List all the supporting arguments both FOR and AGAINST. Then, add the supporting logic and examples for each argument.

FOR

Argument 1
_____
_____
_____

Support
_____
_____
_____

Argument 2
_____
_____
_____

Support
_____
_____
_____

Argument 3
_____
_____
_____

Support
_____
_____
_____

AGAINST

Argument 1
_____
_____
_____

Support
_____
_____
_____

Argument 2
_____
_____
_____

Support
_____
_____
_____

Argument 3
_____
_____
_____

Support
_____
_____
_____

Making Supporting Examples: Facts

A fact is something true. For debates, you can use facts that are common knowledge, but you should also try to use more specific, less commonly known facts. The best places to find specific facts are newspaper and magazine articles. In these sources, you can find all of the details of a situation and can read interviews from people related to the story. Below are some facts related to the topic of banning junk food in schools.

Additional Research

Before starting your argument, let's do some extra research about the topic. Read the facts about school lunches.

■ In 2010, the Healthy, Hunger-Free Kids Act was created. Its purpose is to encourage public schools to follow nutritional guidelines in their cafeteria lunches. Schools that follow the guidelines will receive extra funding. So far, the program has had mixed results. On the one hand, schools have started serving more healthy foods. On the other hand, many schools have not found a way to get their students to eat the healthier meals.

■ One student at a New York City high school complained about the new school lunches. "Before, the school food was not that tasty, but at least they served good foods like pizza and fried chicken. Now, they are making us eat fruits and vegetables, so there are no taste and no flavor, and the food is healthy. This is even worse!" Not surprisingly, many students at this school throw away more food than they eat.

■ Other schools have tried serving more exotic foods to get their students to eat more. In Los Angeles, several schools began serving dishes such as Thai fried rice and Indian curry. Even with these healthy and tasty meals, students still complain. One seventh grader said, "These new foods are too strange for me. And I don't want to eat vegetables. Where're the hamburgers? Where's the ice cream?" However, there is some hope for getting kids to eat more healthy foods. An eighth grade student admitted, "I usually throw away most of the vegetables the school serves," but added, "except for the apples. I really like them."

Work with a partner and answer the following questions. Phrases have been provided to help you.

1 What is the law which changed nutritional guidelines for schools?

→ The act is called _____, and it was created in _____.

2 What is the high school student's opinion of the new school lunches?

→ The student's opinion is _____.

3 What are the changes that schools in Los Angeles made to their menus?

→ In Los Angeles, the schools _____.

4 What is the seventh grader's opinion of the new school lunches?

→ The student feels that _____.

Your Research

Find an article about junk food from a magazine, newspaper, or academic website. Paste or tape the article in your workbook in the space below.

Paste or Tape Your Research Article Here

Use your article and write four specific examples or pieces of evidence you can use for your debate. Try to include different types of examples, including opinion polls, statistics, academic studies, and general facts.

- _____
- _____
- _____
- _____

Debate Note-Taking

Use this page to take notes about the opposing team's arguments during the debate.

Note-Taking

_____
_____
_____
_____
_____
_____
_____
_____
_____
_____

Peer Evaluation

Read the assessment criteria and objectively evaluate your peers on a scale from 1 to 10.

CRITERIA	Name				
Understands the subject well	/10	/10	/10	/10	/10
Supports opinion with clear logic and examples	/10	/10	/10	/10	/10
Introduces opinions with appropriate connectors (In my view, I agree, For example, etc.)	/10	/10	/10	/10	/10
Uses a variety of vocabulary and expressions	/10	/10	/10	/10	/10
Accurately uses a variety of grammatical structures	/10	/10	/10	/10	/10
Does not monopolize the conversation and lets other people express themselves	/10	/10	/10	/10	/10
Listens attentively and respects other people's opinions	/10	/10	/10	/10	/10
Is able to accept criticism without becoming upset	/10	/10	/10	/10	/10
TOTAL SCORE	/80	/80	/80	/80	/80

Unit 04: Animal Testing

Organizing Ideas

Should animals be used in scientific experiments?

Look at the reading passage in your textbook. List all the supporting arguments both FOR and AGAINST. Then, add the supporting logic and examples for each argument.

FOR

Argument 1
_____
_____
_____

Support
_____
_____
_____

Argument 2
_____
_____
_____

Support
_____
_____
_____

Argument 3
_____
_____
_____

Support
_____
_____
_____

AGAINST

Argument 1
_____
_____
_____

Support
_____
_____
_____

Argument 2
_____
_____
_____

Support
_____
_____
_____

Argument 3
_____
_____
_____

Support
_____
_____
_____

Making Supporting Examples: Academic Studies

Academic studies are research that is done by universities, governments, and large research organizations. During these studies, researchers examine events to understand what causes them and why they are important. Using academic studies is a good way to strengthen your argument. Below are some academic studies related to the topic of using animals in scientific experiments.

Additional Research

Before starting your argument, let's do some extra research about the topic. Read the academic studies about animal testing.

The Society Against Animal Testing
A lot of scientists use animals for testing because they believe the results on animals will be similar to the results on human patients. However, it is important to remember that animal testing is not always accurate. Animals have different body structures than we do. These differences may be small, but they can make a huge difference. For instance, rhesus monkeys are often used to test new AIDS medicines. The problem with this is that the monkeys cannot be infected with HIV. Instead, they are infected with SIV. Although the virus is similar to HIV, it is not exactly the same. As a result, we cannot know if a drug tested on the monkeys will work on humans as well. This means it is necessary for scientists to use alternative testing methods that are more accurate. These include stem-cell research and computer models.

The American Physiological Society
One of the greatest difficulties scientists face during testing is controlling variables. In the case of studies on humans, there are too many variables to give accurate test results. For example, everybody has a different diet, keeps his or her home at a different temperature, and gets a different amount of exercise each day. With animals, controlling these variables is much easier. The obvious benefit of this is that results of tests on animals will be more accurate and consistent than tests on humans.

Work with a partner and answer the following questions. Phrases have been provided to help you.

1 According to The Society Against Animal Testing, why is animal testing inaccurate?
   → *It is inaccurate due to the fact that* _____.

2 What is the potential problem of AIDS studies done with rhesus monkeys?
   → *The potential problem is* _____.

3 What are the factors to control in experiments according to the American Physiological Society?
   → *The factors are* _____.

4 In what way are animal experiments better than experiments on human beings?
   → *They are better because* _____.

Your Research

Find an article about animal testing from a magazine, newspaper, or academic website. Paste or tape the article in your workbook in the space below.

Paste or Tape Your Research Article Here

Use your article and write four specific examples or pieces of evidence you can use for your debate. Try to include different types of examples, including opinion polls, statistics, academic studies, and general facts.

- _____
- _____
- _____
- _____

Debate Note-Taking

Use this page to take notes about the opposing team's arguments during the debate.

Note-Taking

_____
_____
_____
_____
_____
_____
_____
_____
_____
_____

Peer Evaluation

Read the assessment criteria and objectively evaluate your peers on a scale from 1 to 10.

CRITERIA	Name				
Understands the subject well	/10	/10	/10	/10	/10
Supports opinion with clear logic and examples	/10	/10	/10	/10	/10
Introduces opinions with appropriate connectors (In my view, I agree, For example, etc.)	/10	/10	/10	/10	/10
Uses a variety of vocabulary and expressions	/10	/10	/10	/10	/10
Accurately uses a variety of grammatical structures	/10	/10	/10	/10	/10
Does not monopolize the conversation and lets other people express themselves	/10	/10	/10	/10	/10
Listens attentively and respects other people's opinions	/10	/10	/10	/10	/10
Is able to accept criticism without becoming upset	/10	/10	/10	/10	/10
TOTAL SCORE	/80	/80	/80	/80	/80

Unit 05: Beauty Pageants

Organizing Ideas

Should beauty pageants be allowed to continue?

Look at the reading passage in your textbook. List all the supporting arguments both FOR and AGAINST. Then, add the supporting logic and examples for each argument.

FOR

Argument 1
_____
_____
_____

Support
_____
_____
_____

Argument 2
_____
_____
_____

Support
_____
_____
_____

Argument 3
_____
_____
_____

Support
_____
_____
_____

AGAINST

Argument 1
_____
_____
_____

Support
_____
_____
_____

Argument 2
_____
_____
_____

Support
_____
_____
_____

Argument 3
_____
_____
_____

Support
_____
_____
_____

Making Supporting Examples: Personal Experience

Personal experience is your experience related to the topic. Using personal experience can be a good way to support your argument if you explain how your experience proves your point. However, you should be careful because one person's experience might not be common. This can actually weaken your argument. Below are some personal experiences related to the topic of beauty pageants.

Additional Research

Before starting your argument, let's do some extra research about the topic. Read the personal experience about beauty pageants.

> The following is part of an interview with beauty pageant contestant Lisa Gomez.
>
> **Q:** *How did joining the beauty pageant make you feel?*
>
> **Lisa:** Joining the pageant made me feel more confident in myself. Of course, it also made me more popular in school. It also inspired me to get involved with extracurricular activities such as my school's dance team.
>
> **Q:** *What are some of the pros and cons of participating in a beauty contest?*
>
> **Lisa:** The main pros would definitely be making new friends and strengthening your personality. By joining a pageant, contestants have to learn how to stay calm under pressure. But I would say this is actually one of the downsides. These pageants are very competitive, and a lot of participants can't take the pressure. Also, with every winner, there are losers. People who lose in the competition often go home broken hearted.
>
> **Q:** *Would you recommend participating in beauty pageants to your friends? Why?*
>
> **Lisa:** Yes, definitely! Pageants teach us lessons about ourselves and interacting with others that we cannot learn inside the classroom. These are skills that we can use throughout our lives.

Work with a partner and answer the following questions. Phrases have been provided to help you.

1 How did participating in the beauty pageant affect Lisa's school life?

→ *It affected her school life in that she* _____.

2 What are the pros of beauty contests according to Lisa?

→ *According to Lisa, the pros of beauty contests are* _____.

3 What are the cons of beauty contests according to Lisa?

→ *According to Lisa, the cons of beauty contests are* _____.

4 Why does Lisa recommend participating in beauty pageants?

→ *She recommends it because* _____.

Your Research

Find an article about beauty pageants from a magazine, newspaper, or academic website. Paste or tape the article in your workbook in the space below.

Paste or Tape Your Research Article Here

Use your article and write four specific examples or pieces of evidence you can use for your debate. Try to include different types of examples, including opinion polls, statistics, academic studies, and general facts.

- _____
- _____
- _____
- _____

Debate Note-Taking

Use this page to take notes about the opposing team's arguments during the debate.

Note-Taking

_____
_____
_____
_____
_____
_____
_____
_____
_____
_____

Peer Evaluation

Read the assessment criteria and objectively evaluate your peers on a scale from 1 to 10.

CRITERIA	Name				
Understands the subject well	/10	/10	/10	/10	/10
Supports opinion with clear logic and examples	/10	/10	/10	/10	/10
Introduces opinions with appropriate connectors (In my view, I agree, For example, etc.)	/10	/10	/10	/10	/10
Uses a variety of vocabulary and expressions	/10	/10	/10	/10	/10
Accurately uses a variety of grammatical structures	/10	/10	/10	/10	/10
Does not monopolize the conversation and lets other people express themselves	/10	/10	/10	/10	/10
Listens attentively and respects other people's opinions	/10	/10	/10	/10	/10
Is able to accept criticism without becoming upset	/10	/10	/10	/10	/10
TOTAL SCORE	/80	/80	/80	/80	/80

Unit 06 Violent Video Games

Organizing Ideas

Should violent video games be allowed for sale?

Look at the reading passage in your textbook. List all the supporting arguments both FOR and AGAINST. Then, add the supporting logic and examples for each argument.

FOR	AGAINST
Argument 1	**Argument 1**
Support	**Support**
Argument 2	**Argument 2**
Support	**Support**
Argument 3	**Argument 3**
Support	**Support**

Making Supporting Examples: Statistics

Statistics are facts based on numbers. They are usually created by governments, universities, news organizations, and companies. Statistics often show the number of people, companies, and nations that agree with a certain opinion or policy. To show these numbers, statistics can include percentages, populations, and points. Below are some statistics related to the topic of violent video games.

Additional Research

Before starting your argument, let's do some extra research about the topic. Read the statistics about violent video games.

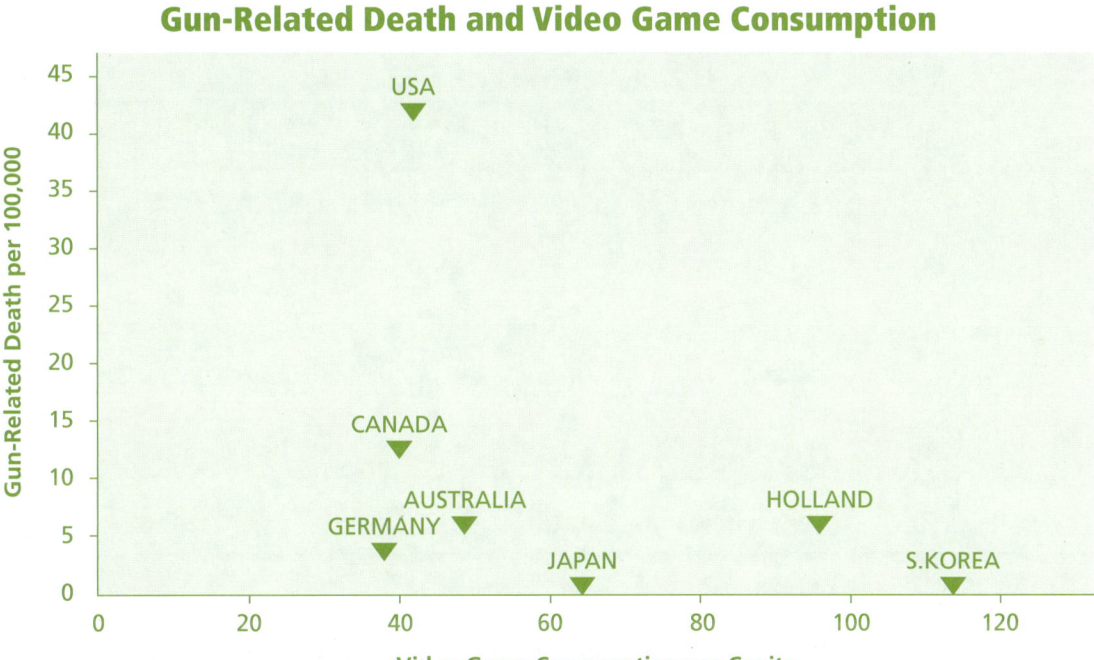

Work with a partner and answer the following questions. Phrases have been provided to help you.

1 Which country has the highest number of gun-related deaths per people?
   → *According to this graph,* _____.

2 Which countries have no gun-related deaths?
   → *The countries which have no gun-related deaths are* _____.

3 Which three countries have the most video game players?
   → *The three countries are* _____.

4 What is the overall message of this chart?
   → *The overall message of this chart is* _____.

Your Research

Find an article about violent video games from a magazine, newspaper, or academic website. Paste or tape the article in your workbook in the space below.

Paste or Tape Your Research Article Here

Use your article and write four specific examples or pieces of evidence you can use for your debate. Try to include different types of examples, including opinion polls, statistics, academic studies, and general facts.

- _____
- _____
- _____
- _____

Debate Note-Taking

Use this page to take notes about the opposing team's arguments during the debate.

Note-Taking

Peer Evaluation

Read the assessment criteria and objectively evaluate your peers on a scale from 1 to 10.

CRITERIA	Name				
Understands the subject well	/10	/10	/10	/10	/10
Supports opinion with clear logic and examples	/10	/10	/10	/10	/10
Introduces opinions with appropriate connectors (In my view, I agree, For example, etc.)	/10	/10	/10	/10	/10
Uses a variety of vocabulary and expressions	/10	/10	/10	/10	/10
Accurately uses a variety of grammatical structures	/10	/10	/10	/10	/10
Does not monopolize the conversation and lets other people express themselves	/10	/10	/10	/10	/10
Listens attentively and respects other people's opinions	/10	/10	/10	/10	/10
Is able to accept criticism without becoming upset	/10	/10	/10	/10	/10
TOTAL SCORE	/80	/80	/80	/80	/80

Unit 07: Giving Children Allowances

Organizing Ideas

Should parents give their children allowances?

Look at the reading passage in your textbook. List all the supporting arguments both FOR and AGAINST. Then, add the supporting logic and examples for each argument.

FOR	AGAINST
Argument 1	**Argument 1**
Support	**Support**
Argument 2	**Argument 2**
Support	**Support**
Argument 3	**Argument 3**
Support	**Support**

Making Supporting Examples: Expert Opinions

Expert opinions are usually the ideas and opinions of experts in a given field. Experts are typically people such as professors, doctors, and business managers. Most experts base their opinions on their years of experience doing researching and working in their fields. Below are some expert opinions related to the topic of giving children allowances.

Additional Research

Before starting your argument, let's do some extra research about the topic. Read the expert opinions about giving children allowance.

Julie Gatwick, editor at a personal finance magazine

As a parent, should you give an allowance to your children? Absolutely! But it is essential that you teach your children a lesson about money in the process. The most important lesson is about saving money. There are some kids who will save their money no matter what. Other times, though, the kids want to spend and spend. If this is the case with your child, there are a couple of steps you must take. First, you must define how much you want the child to save. Talk to your child and decide on a reasonable amount to save—say maybe 15 to 25 percent of each allowance. Also, you should try to make saving fun. Put the money in a piggy bank, for instance, so your child can actually see his or her money growing. When your children save enough money, help them make their own purchases. This way, they can see themselves being rewarded.

Alice Jones, child psychologist

As a mother of three, I agree that parents should help their children learn important life lessons. This is definitely true of money. In the case of younger children—those under the age of 12 or so—I feel that other lessons are more important. Younger children can understand the concept of money, but they really don't have a need for it in their daily lives. At this young age, parents generally provide everything for their children. This is really for the best. At such a young age, it is better for children to learn about forming friendships, doing well in school, and eating healthy foods. Learning about money is a lesson better saved for later teenage years and early adulthood. At that time, your children will have a better idea of what they need to use money for.

Work with a partner and answer the following questions. Phrases have been provided to help you.

1 According to Julie Gatwick, what is the first step parents should take to help their children save?
   → *Gatwick says parents should* _____.

2 What system does Gatwick suggest to help children save for larger purchases?
   → *The system she suggests is* _____.

3 What does Alice Jones believe about teaching children about money?
   → *She believes that* _____.

4 Why does Jones suggest teaching children about money when they are older?
   → *She suggests this because* _____.

Your Research

Find an article about giving children allowances from a magazine, newspaper, or academic website. Paste or tape the article in your workbook in the space below.

Paste or Tape Your Research Article Here

Use your article and write four specific examples or pieces of evidence you can use for your debate. Try to include different types of examples, including opinion polls, statistics, academic studies, and general facts.

- _____
- _____
- _____
- _____

Debate Note-Taking

Use this page to take notes about the opposing team's arguments during the debate.

Note-Taking

Peer Evaluation

Read the assessment criteria and objectively evaluate your peers on a scale from 1 to 10.

CRITERIA	Name				
Understands the subject well	/10	/10	/10	/10	/10
Supports opinion with clear logic and examples	/10	/10	/10	/10	/10
Introduces opinions with appropriate connectors (In my view, I agree, For example, etc.)	/10	/10	/10	/10	/10
Uses a variety of vocabulary and expressions	/10	/10	/10	/10	/10
Accurately uses a variety of grammatical structures	/10	/10	/10	/10	/10
Does not monopolize the conversation and lets other people express themselves	/10	/10	/10	/10	/10
Listens attentively and respects other people's opinions	/10	/10	/10	/10	/10
Is able to accept criticism without becoming upset	/10	/10	/10	/10	/10
TOTAL SCORE	/80	/80	/80	/80	/80

Unit 08 Elementary School Uniforms

Organizing Ideas

Should elementary schools also require school uniforms?

Look at the reading passage in your textbook. List all the supporting arguments both FOR and AGAINST. Then, add the supporting logic and examples for each argument.

FOR	AGAINST
Argument 1	**Argument 1**
Support	**Support**
Argument 2	**Argument 2**
Support	**Support**
Argument 3	**Argument 3**
Support	**Support**

Making Supporting Examples: Facts

A fact is something true. For debates, you can use facts that are common knowledge, but you should also try to use more specific, less commonly known facts. The best places to find specific facts are newspaper and magazine articles. In these sources, you can find all of the details of a situation and can read interviews from people related to the story. Below are some facts related to the topic of requiring school uniforms.

Additional Research

Before starting your argument, let's do some extra research about the topic. Read the facts about school uniforms.

> **Newspaper Article:** *Do Uniforms Really Boost Student Academic Performance?*
>
> If you look at the school uniform situation in the United States, you will find that private schools and "at-risk" public schools in poor urban areas require school uniforms. But what about the schools with the highest test scores? Do they also require their students to wear school uniforms? Oftentimes, the answer is no. For instance, one of the highest-ranked schools in the state of Illinois is Allenton Elementary School, located just outside Chicago. At Allenton, students are allowed to wear whatever clothes they want. In spite of this, the students at Allenton consistently get some of the highest test scores in the state. Last year, the school was ranked number two.
>
> So if uniforms are not the solution to higher academic performance, what is? Evidence shows that parents and the overall community play the largest roles. In schools like Allenton, parents, teachers, and students all work hard to reach their academic goals. Even from a young age, the children understand the importance of education in their lives. They are unlikely to be distracted by school violence, gangs, and other problems that inner-city schools must deal with. On the contrary, students at these schools are surrounded by positive role models. Their parents have professional jobs and seriously value education. These values get transferred to their children.

Work with a partner and answer the following questions. Phrases have been provided to help you.

1 Which schools in the United States usually have school uniform requirements?

→ *The schools in the United States that require uniforms are* _____.

2 What is the relationship between successful public schools and school uniforms?

→ *The relationship is* _____.

3 What factors contribute more to higher academic performance than uniforms?

→ *The factors that contribute more are* _____.

4 Why are students at the top schools more academically successful?

→ *These students are successful because* _____.

Your Research

Find an article about requiring school uniforms from a magazine, newspaper, or academic website. Paste or tape the article in your workbook in the space below.

Use your article and write four specific examples or pieces of evidence you can use for your debate. Try to include different types of examples, including opinion polls, statistics, academic studies, and general facts.

- _____
  _____
- _____
  _____
- _____
  _____
- _____
  _____

Debate Note-Taking

Use this page to take notes about the opposing team's arguments during the debate.

Note-Taking

_____
_____
_____
_____
_____
_____
_____
_____
_____
_____
_____

Peer Evaluation

Read the assessment criteria and objectively evaluate your peers on a scale from 1 to 10.

CRITERIA	Name				
Understands the subject well	/10	/10	/10	/10	/10
Supports opinion with clear logic and examples	/10	/10	/10	/10	/10
Introduces opinions with appropriate connectors (In my view, I agree, For example, etc.)	/10	/10	/10	/10	/10
Uses a variety of vocabulary and expressions	/10	/10	/10	/10	/10
Accurately uses a variety of grammatical structures	/10	/10	/10	/10	/10
Does not monopolize the conversation and lets other people express themselves	/10	/10	/10	/10	/10
Listens attentively and respects other people's opinions	/10	/10	/10	/10	/10
Is able to accept criticism without becoming upset	/10	/10	/10	/10	/10
TOTAL SCORE	/80	/80	/80	/80	/80

Unit 09: English as the World Language

Organizing Ideas

Should everybody in the world speak English?

Look at the reading passage in your textbook. List all the supporting arguments both FOR and AGAINST. Then, add the supporting logic and examples for each argument.

FOR

Argument 1
_____
_____
_____

Support
_____
_____
_____

Argument 2
_____
_____
_____

Support
_____
_____
_____

Argument 3
_____
_____
_____

Support
_____
_____
_____

AGAINST

Argument 1
_____
_____
_____

Support
_____
_____
_____

Argument 2
_____
_____
_____

Support
_____
_____
_____

Argument 3
_____
_____
_____

Support
_____
_____
_____

Making Supporting Examples: Academic Studies

Academic studies are research that is done by universities, governments, and large research organizations. During these studies, researchers examine events to understand what causes them and why they are important. Using academic studies is a good way to strengthen your argument. Below are some academic studies related to the topic of using English as a world language.

Additional Research

Before starting your argument, let's do some extra research about the topic. Read the expert opinions about using English as a world language.

Center for Economic Policy and Development

English is well on its way to becoming the dominant global language. Is this a good thing? For business and science, it absolutely is. Having a common language makes work in these areas more efficient. However, the dominance of English is bad news for literature. Consider the following points:

Language Matters in Literature

For science and business, using only English is not a problem because the main goal is communication. The language does not matter. With literature, the language is part of the experience. A novel uses wordplay, puns, metaphors, and other characteristics of the language it is written in to give more meaning.

Very Few Authors Have Written in Multiple Languages

Very few famous authors in history have written in more than one language. Two of them are Samuel Beckett and Vladimir Vladimirovich Nabokov. Most other authors in history have always used their native language to write novels. The reason was that writing in their native language allowed them to express themselves most clearly and freely.

Work with a partner and answer the following questions. Phrases have been provided to help you.

1. Why is having English the dominant language good for business and science?
   → *It is good because* _____.

2. Why does language matter more with literature?
   → *It matters more because* _____.

3. What are some features of a language that novelists often use?
   → *Some features novelists often use are* _____.

4. Why do authors usually only write in their native language?
   → *They do this because* _____.

Your Research

Find an article about using English as a world language from a magazine, newspaper, or academic website. Paste or tape the article in your workbook in the space below.

Paste or Tape Your Research Article Here

Use your article and write four specific examples or pieces of evidence you can use for your debate. Try to include different types of examples, including opinion polls, statistics, academic studies, and general facts.

- _____
- _____
- _____
- _____

Debate Note-Taking

Use this page to take notes about the opposing team's arguments during the debate.

Note-Taking

_____

_____

_____

_____

_____

_____

_____

_____

_____

_____

_____

Peer Evaluation

Read the assessment criteria and objectively evaluate your peers on a scale from 1 to 10.

CRITERIA	Name				
Understands the subject well	/10	/10	/10	/10	/10
Supports opinion with clear logic and examples	/10	/10	/10	/10	/10
Introduces opinions with appropriate connectors (In my view, I agree, For example, etc.)	/10	/10	/10	/10	/10
Uses a variety of vocabulary and expressions	/10	/10	/10	/10	/10
Accurately uses a variety of grammatical structures	/10	/10	/10	/10	/10
Does not monopolize the conversation and lets other people express themselves	/10	/10	/10	/10	/10
Listens attentively and respects other people's opinions	/10	/10	/10	/10	/10
Is able to accept criticism without becoming upset	/10	/10	/10	/10	/10
TOTAL SCORE	/80	/80	/80	/80	/80

Unit 10: Social Networking Sites for Education

Organizing Ideas

Should social networking sites be used in education?

Look at the reading passage in your textbook. List all the supporting arguments both FOR and AGAINST. Then, add the supporting logic and examples for each argument.

FOR

Argument 1
_____
_____
_____

Support
_____
_____
_____

Argument 2
_____
_____
_____

Support
_____
_____
_____

Argument 3
_____
_____
_____

Support
_____
_____
_____

AGAINST

Argument 1
_____
_____
_____

Support
_____
_____
_____

Argument 2
_____
_____
_____

Support
_____
_____
_____

Argument 3
_____
_____
_____

Support
_____
_____
_____

Making Supporting Examples: Personal Experience

Personal experience is your experience related to the topic. Using personal experience can be a good way to support your argument if you explain how your experience proves your point. However, you should be careful because one person's experience might not be common. This can actually weaken your argument. Below are some personal experiences related to the topic of using social networking sites for education.

Additional Research

Before starting your argument, let's do some extra research about the topic. Read the personal experiences about using social networking sites for education.

Sally Green, an American middle school teacher:
"This year, I have tried to use social networking sites in my class. I must say that it has not been the perfect solution I'd hoped it would be. On the positive side, students participate more on their schoolwork. For example, I posted a Facebook message asking students to name their favorite president. All but one of my students did so. This sounds great until you get to the second part. I asked them to explain why they liked that president. Nearly all of them copied and pasted part of the Wikipedia article about that president. So for my class, social networking sites have gotten more students to participate. It's just the lack of creativity that I'm worried about."

Brandon Jones, a Canadian high school student:
"In my opinion, social networking sites are the best way to help students learn. Students like me spend a lot of time on social networking sites every day. What could be better than getting students to learn by using social networking sites? For my literature class, my teacher asked us to make a presentation about the book we read: *The Great Gatsby*. My classmates and I decided to make a short play using a scene from the book. We made a video of it and uploaded it to YouTube. Not only did we get an A on the project, but our video was also seen by thousands of people. Using social networking sites is a great way to help students learn."

Work with a partner and answer the following questions. Phrases have been provided to help you.

1 How has Ms. Green benefitted from using social networking sites in her class?

→ *Ms. Green has benefitted from* _____.

2 What problem did Ms. Green have with her students' work on social networking sites?

→ *The problem she had was* _____.

3 How did Brandon use social networking sites for his schoolwork?

→ *Brandon used social networking sites to* _____.

4 What was the result when he used social networking sites for his project?

→ *The result was* _____.

Your Research

Find an article about using social networking sites for education from a magazine, newspaper, or academic website. Paste or tape the article in your workbook in the space below.

Use your article and write four specific examples or pieces of evidence you can use for your debate. Try to include different types of examples, including opinion polls, statistics, academic studies, and general facts.

- _____
- _____
- _____
- _____

Debate Note-Taking

Use this page to take notes about the opposing team's arguments during the debate.

Note-Taking

_____
_____
_____
_____
_____
_____
_____
_____
_____
_____

Peer Evaluation

Read the assessment criteria and objectively evaluate your peers on a scale from 1 to 10.

CRITERIA	Name				
Understands the subject well	/10	/10	/10	/10	/10
Supports opinion with clear logic and examples	/10	/10	/10	/10	/10
Introduces opinions with appropriate connectors (In my view, I agree, For example, etc.)	/10	/10	/10	/10	/10
Uses a variety of vocabulary and expressions	/10	/10	/10	/10	/10
Accurately uses a variety of grammatical structures	/10	/10	/10	/10	/10
Does not monopolize the conversation and lets other people express themselves	/10	/10	/10	/10	/10
Listens attentively and respects other people's opinions	/10	/10	/10	/10	/10
Is able to accept criticism without becoming upset	/10	/10	/10	/10	/10
TOTAL SCORE	/80	/80	/80	/80	/80

Memo

Memo

DEBATE Pro
Book 1
Workbook